Not Just for the Money

Not Just for the Money

An Economic Theory of Personal Motivation

Bruno S. Frey

Professor of Economics, University of Zurich, Switzerland

Edward Elgar
Cheltenham UK • Northampton, MA, USA

Published by
Edward Elgar Publishing Limited
Glensanda House
Montpellier Parade
Cheltenham
Glos GL50 1UA
UK

Edward Elgar Publishing, Inc.
136 West Street
Suite 202
Northampton
Massachusetts 01060
USA

Paperback edition printed 1998
Paperback edition reprinted 2000

This book has been printed on demand to keep the title in print.

A catalogue record for this book
is available from the British Library

Library of Congress Cataloguing in Publication Data
Frey, Bruno S.
    Not just for the money : an economic theory of personal motivation
    / Bruno Frey.
    Includes bibliographical references and index.
    1. Employee motivation.   2. Performance.   I. Title.
    HF5549.5.M63F74   1997   96–35154
                                                                            CIP

ISBN   978-1-85898-509-1 (cased)
        978-1-85898-845-0 (paperback)

Typeset by Manton Typesetters, 5–7 Eastfield Road, Louth, Lincolnshire LN11 7AJ, UK

Contents

Tables and Figures

TABLES

FIGURES

Preface

Do people act just because they expect a monetary gain? Do they work solely because they are paid? I claim that this is not so: people undertake many activities simply because they like them.

I claim even more: a higher monetary compensation crowds-out this inner motivation in important circumstances. To offer higher pay then makes people less committed to their work, and may reduce their performance.

These views are at odds with conventional economics. *Not Just for the Money* develops an economic theory of human motivation which is at the same time broader and, in relevant cases, contradictory to economics teaching. Human motivation is not restricted to monetary incentives. In addition to the *extrinsic motivation* induced from outside, *intrinsic motivation* is also crucially important. People do things by intrinsic motivation when they just enjoy doing them, such as playing cards with friends the whole night, jogging for miles, climbing high mountains, spending hours solving crossword puzzles, contributing anonymously to a charitable organization, or working without compensation in a developing country's hospital. Intrinsic motivation goes, however, far beyond such partial examples.

Five basic propositions characterizing the relationship between intrinsic and extrinsic motivation are advanced in this book:

(1) Intrinsic motivation is of *great importance* for all economic activities. It is inconceivable that people are motivated solely or even mainly by external incentives.
(2) The use of monetary incentives *crowds out* intrinsic motivation under identifiable and relevant conditions (*Crowding-Out Effect*).
(3) Other *external interventions* such as commands or regulations can drive out intrinsic motivation.
(4) External interventions may *enhance* intrinsic motivation under some conditions (*Crowding-In Effect*).
(5) Changes in intrinsic motivations may spill over to areas not

directly affected by monetary incentives or regulations (*Spill-Over Effect*).

In the following, these propositions will be fully explained, put into the context of economic and psychological theory, and empirically documented. The book proceeds by first establishing the Crowding-Out Effect (as well as its opposite, the Crowding-In Effect) and the motivational Spill-Over Effect (Part I). A large number of applications to constitutional questions, various policy issues, and the organization of firms are provided in Part II. Part III discusses the substantial consequences for policy making and for economic theory. A modified model of human behaviour – called '*Homo Oeconomicus Maturus*' or *HOM* – is presented.

This is *not* a tract against the market or against the price system. Such an interpretation would be wrong for three reasons:

(a) The (relative) Price Effect which captures the price system's essential mechanism is fully accepted. The Crowding-Out Effect introduced here is an *additional* force working in exactly the *opposite direction*: a higher monetary reward offered may reduce an activity instead of increasing it.

(b) Intrinsic motivation is only crowded-out by external interventions under *specific* conditions. In impersonal and purely abstract interactions – such as trading on the electronic stock market or paying for bread in the supermarket – there is no Crowding-Out Effect and the Price Effect works as envisaged by Adam Smith and traditional economic theory. This book contends, however, that the economy is not restricted to such large, impersonal markets. Quite the contrary: most economic dealings on goods markets, and even more so on labour markets, are not so abstract and are therefore subject to Crowding-Out Effects.

(c) As intrinsic motivation is crowded out by monetary incentives as well as by regulations, the policy solution is certainly not to substitute government intervention for markets. Often, the opposite is advisable because the Crowding-Out Effect is stronger with direct interventions by command than with more indirect interventions via pricing.

The economic policy recommendations deviate both from naive 'marketeering' and naive 'interventionism'. Rather, an important limit to both of them is shown. It is argued that human beings should be trusted and that one should rely – where appropriate – on their intrinsic motivation. Desist from trying to steer humans everywhere and always; leave room for the *Homo Oeconomicus Maturus*.

The ideas included in this book have taken many years to form. I was first confronted to what finally became the Crowding-Out Effect in a small interdisciplinary group of scholars which has met regularly for the past twelve years. I am particularly grateful to psychologists Kurt Stapf (University of Tübingen), Wolfgang Stroebe (University of Utrecht) and Klaus Foppa (University of Berne) for making me aware of the 'hidden cost of reward'. While I was immediately struck by this 'strange' effect going against all I as an economist knew about human behaviour, I did not immediately grasp its full relevance.

Over the years I had extensive discussions about the Crowding-Out and Spill-Over Effects with friends and co-workers, too many to mention here. But I explicitly wish to mention the most stimulating and critical interaction with my assistants and co-workers at the University of Zurich: an earlier group comprising especially Hannelore Weck-Hannemann, Beat Gygi and Angel Serna (the latter two are now editorial writers with the leading Swiss newspaper Neue Zürcher Zeitung); and the present group, most importantly Reiner Eichenberger, Iris Bohnet, and Felix Oberholzer-Gee (who is a co-author of one of the chapters).

The ideas slowly ripened when I presented them at many different conferences and university seminars in Europe, North and South America. Of special importance were two conferences: one at the Reimers Stiftung in Bad Homburg (organized by Karl-Dieter Opp, Siegwart Lindenberg and Michael Hechter), and guided by the much lamented James Coleman; another at the Humboldt University in Berlin (organized by Joachim Schwalbach and Harry Barkema) where I had the chance to present my views on the consequences of the Crowding-Out Effect for the compensation of managers to organization and business economics specialists. I have also benefited much from a joint psychology–economics seminar with Dieter Frey and his co-workers from the Universities of Munich and Kiel, a joint seminar with my brother René L. Frey and his assistants at the University of Basle, and one with Hansjörg Siegenthaler, Margit Osterloh and Ernst Fehr and their co-workers at my University in Zurich. I am particularly grateful to Margit Osterloh who has enlightened me on the business economics aspects.

At these conferences and seminars I received a large number of challenging comments. I certainly could not convince all my economics colleagues that there is not only a Price Effect but that it has to be amended by the Crowding-Out Effect – but perhaps the idea is too unorthodox for many economists to accept.

I also profited greatly from various extended stays at foreign universities. The most important has been as a visiting research professor at the Graduate School of Business of the University of Chicago. I was much challenged by the late George Stigler, and much supported, encouraged and helped by Gary Becker, who also arranged for me to spend some months as a visiting scholar at the Hoover Institution of Stanford University. Oliver Williamson, Daniel Rubinfeld and Bob Cooper made it possible for me to stay various times in the stimulating atmosphere of the University of California at Berkeley. One version of this book was completed while I was a visitor at the Center of Economic Studies of the University of Munich.

Crowding-Out theory and its applications to specific topics over the years found their way into various academic journals, among them the *Journal of Political Economy, Kyklos, Rationality and Society, Journal des Economistes et des Etudes Humaines, Journal of Economic Psychology, European Economic Review, Environmental and Resource Economics*, and *Economic Inquiry*. While the book partly draws on the material contained therein, the chapters have been totally rewritten and many additional parts have been added. The research was in part financially supported by the Swiss National Fund in the context of a project on 'The Limits of the Price System' (No. 12-42480.94).

I am most grateful to my co-workers Reiner Eichenberger, Iris Bohnet, Felix Oberholzer-Gee, Jürg de Spindler, Marcel Kucher and Isabelle Busenhart for helping me to write this book. They continually stimulated me, and proved again and again the productivity of intellectual exchange and open discussion – the value of an 'academic republic'.

Bruno S. Frey

1. Introduction: The market and beyond

The use of prices to foster supply, ration demand and to bring them into equilibrium belongs to the major innovations of mankind. It is no simple step to move from personalized and good-specific barter to the abstract price system which moreover is completely devoid of morale. Those societies, who have understood the efficiency of the price mechanism, have become rich quite independently of their other characteristics. Markets have made the medieval north Italian towns rich, have helped Germany and Japan to become prosperous after a devastating war, and have enabled today's Asian tigers Hong Kong, Taiwan, Singapore, and increasingly South Korea, Thailand and Malaysia, to join the developed economies.

Despite this huge success, markets are often not well understood and are sometimes rejected. Surprisingly, many are still attracted by the communist experiment which ended in a catastrophe not only in terms of the abominably low income of the population but also in terms of a widespread destruction of the environment. What makes this ideology still superior to markets is the underlying concept of 'socialist man' who is supposed to be motivated to work for society as a whole and does not need any lowly monetary incentives to function. This function is widespread also in (so-called) market economies of the Western type. The use of the price system is often strongly rejected, and traditional or bureaucratic means are preferred. In a recent survey (Frey and Pommerehne, 1993) among 1750 households in Switzerland and Germany, we asked whether a price increase in a situation where demand clearly exceeds supply was considered 'fair' or 'unfair'. The specific question asked reads (in translation):

A hardware store has been selling snow shovels for 30 Swiss Francs (or 30 German Marks). The morning after a heavy snow storm, the store raises the price to CHF/DM 40. How do you evaluate this price rise?

1

Only 17 per cent of the respondents found the rationing of excess demand by raising the price to be 'fair', and not less than 83 per cent found it 'unfair'. A large majority thus rejected the use of pricing in that instance. This feeling is not specific for Europe; virtually the same result was earlier found in a Canadian study (Kahneman, Knetsch and Thaler, 1986a and b). The Swiss/German inquiry found moreover that 76 per cent of the respondents accepted a traditional allocation via the principle of 'first come, first served' to be fair, and 43 per cent favoured an allocation by the public administration. These results indicate that the price system is not as well established in people's thinking as economists like to believe. This helps to explain why pricing is still not used in areas where it would seem to work very well such as, for instance, road pricing.

In strong contrast to these observations on the intellectual level, and in much political and public discourse, there is a 'new orthodoxy' favouring the use of prices. All too often solutions are sought by using markets and perfect competition. Liberalization and privatization tend to be offered as solutions to all problems, especially in formerly planned economy communist countries, but also in developing countries. The only barrier is practicability. It is thus argued: 'If only the countries of the 3rd and 4th world adopted markets, and did so uncompromisingly, they would develop and prosper'. And many editorial writers suggest for industrial countries: 'If everything were left to pricing, we would be near to Nirvana'.

This 'new market orthodoxy' by far stretches the limits in which the price system is an effective and useful social decision-making mechanism. However, this book certainly does not turn back to the old adversity against the market so well described by Hirschman (1977, 1982). Nor does it deal with the classical limits of markets in the form of external effects and economies of scale leading to monopolization. Rather, a neglected behavioural motive beyond monetary incentives, intrinsic motivation, is attributed its proper role. It is not claimed that it is *possible* to run an economy based on purely intrinsic incentives. Nor is it argued that the use of intrinsic motivation is always *desirable*. The message is that the exclusive reliance on monetary incentives as suggested by modern economics (and in particular by principal–agent theory) is mistaken. It is indeed neither possible nor desirable to build a society solely or even mainly on monetary incentives – nor, of course, on commands and regulations. *Tertium Datur*: Pricing and regulating are not the only way to run a society. There is in addition intrinsic motivation which under many circumstances is crowded-out by using prices and regulations. This book deals with the relationship between these motivating forces, and seeks to establish under what conditions each one is appropriate.

NOTE

1. Among strong believers in the price system these are not effective limits. They argue that external effects can be overcome by defining property rights which then lead to an efficient allocation of resources via the Coase theorem. Monopolies are not seen as a problem but rather as the result of more profitable, and therefore socially more beneficial, activity.

SUGGESTED FURTHER READINGS

A broad presentation of the price system and other social decision-making mechanism is
Dahl, Robert A. and Charles Lindblom (1953), *Politics, Economics and Welfare*, New York: Harper.
Though this book is rather old, it still gives an excellent survey. A good modern treatment is
Lane, Robert E. (1991), *The Market Experience*, Cambridge: Cambridge University Press.
An analysis of the market and competing governmental systems from the transaction cost viewpoint is provided by
Williamson, Oliver E. (1991), 'Comparative Economic Organization: The Analysis of Discrete Structural Alternatives', *Administrative Science Quarterly*, **36**, 269–96.
Attitudes towards the price system are evaluated in
Frey, Bruno S. (1992), *Economics as a Science of Human Behaviour. Towards a New Social Science Paradigm*, Boston and Dordrecht: Kluwer, ch. 10: The Price System and Morals.
A typical representative of the 'new market orthodoxy' is
Friedman, Milton (1962), *Capitalism and Freedom*, Chicago: Chicago University Press.
Evaluations of the market over the course of history are treated in
Hirschman, Albert O. (1977), *The Passions and the Interests: Political Arguments for Capitalism before its Triumph*, Princeton: Princeton University Press.

PART I
The Crowding-Out Effect

2. Everyday experiences

I MONEY DOES NOT ALWAYS WORK

Imagine the following situation:

> A boy on good terms with his parents willingly mows the lawn of the family home. His father then offers to pay him money each time he cuts the lawn (Case 1).

What will be the result? Most probably, the boy will go on mowing the lawn as long as his father's payment comes forth. But he is not prepared to do any other type of housework for free.

It can indeed be observed that within intact families, the use of monetary compensations for specific services is rare. This also holds for the services the wife renders to her husband, and the husband to his wife. The following account is more typical:

> A girl is given a bicycle by her father because she has been helpful in the house, for instance by mowing the lawn (Case 1A).

It can be expected that such an unspecific payment (a compensation not contingent on having performed a particular service) leads the girl to be glad to perform the housework.

Case 1 and 1A are not restricted to the family. Conditions in which monetary payments may backfire also refer to an increasingly important part of society, namely the voluntary sector. To offer money to a volunteer at the wrong moment and circumstance means that she or he is deeply offended and will discontinue her or his contribution.

> You have been invited to your friend's home for dinner, and he has prepared a wonderful meal. Before you leave, you take out your purse and give your friend an appropriate sum of money (Case 2).

Who in the world would behave this way? Probably nobody in his right mind because virtually everyone knows that this would mean the end of the friendship. By paying, the relationship based on benevolence is basically transformed; if it survives at all, it is then a commercial one which all the people involved interpret quite differently.

There is indeed one man who would not hesitate to pay his friend for dinner: classical *Homo Oeconomicus*. He reckons that the most efficient way to compensate him for the service rendered is in monetary terms. (The interesting thing is that economists subscribing to this notion of man would not commit this drastic mistake. But normally they are not aware of this inconsistency because they have learnt neatly to separate economic theory from real life.)

Consider now Case 2A:

> You go to a restaurant and at the end of the meal, you pay for the services received.

Obviously, the use of monetary compensation does not lead to any problem in this case. On the contrary, the owner will bid you a friendly goodbye and wish that you return.

II ... NOR DOES REGULATING

Take now particularly rational people (so it is said), university professors (Case 3):

> Some professors at a (state) university who are particularly engaged in their profession teach more than the required eight hours per week. Some professors, however, disregard this duty and teach less than required. The ministry of education issues a general regulation whereby the teaching hours of all professors are tightly controlled.

What is likely to happen? It can be expected (the author has circumstantial evidence in this respect) that the particularly engaged professors react by reducing their teaching hours to the minimum required. Capable university administrators are aware of the underlying problem. They make an effort not to issue and enforce across-the-board regulations affecting equally the strongly engaged and the lazy, but seek to monitor the ones with low motivation only. This is in line with Case 3A:

Some university professors are elected by the ministry of education to form an official delegation to attend an important conference meeting in an attractive city.

It would be difficult to see why such an intervention from above should decrease work effort. On the contrary, the selection will be taken as a sign of appreciation, and the respective professors tend to work even harder.

Consider finally the following situation, in which some of us have certainly found ourselves in the past (Case 4):

A friend promises to pick you up at the station when you visit him in the countryside. When you arrive, he is not there but a woman unknown to you tells you that 'your friend has asked me to pick you up because he is prevented'.

You find yourself in an awkward situation. Should you pay the woman for picking you up or not? If she is your friend's friend, offering money would be offensive, and you would possibly run into deep trouble with your friend. If she is not a friend of your friend but a (professional) taxi driver, then you have to pay her. Leaving this to your friend to do afterwards, is again offensive. Most people are fully aware of the pitfalls involved. The best thing probably is to start a conversation with the driver in order to find out whether she is your friend's friend or not.

The cases presented just serve as illustrative examples designed to draw the reader's attention as far as possible on personal experience. As will be shown in this book, the problems identified are directly relevant for a wide range of socio-economic issues. In environmental policy, for instance, the use of monetary payments (such as environmental charges or environmental licenses) to preserve and improve the quality of nature backfires if the love for the environment which people have (environmental morale) is therewith harmed. Paying for blood or for other social services offered in order to help sick and disadvantaged members of society runs the danger of undermining the very motivation for doing so. The same unfortunate outcome is looming when commands (regulations) are introduced in areas of voluntary and charitable work. Specifically compensating an employee, and in particular managers, for tasks which are generally taken to belong to the job (so-called performance-payment), is likely to substitute self-determined by outside-determined work, and therewith reduce personal involvement, creativity and effort. The problems illustrated by these examples refer also to the basic organization of society: a constitution which assumes that all the citizens want to exploit the state, and therefore imposes strict monitoring, controls and duties, destroys citizens' civic virtue. One of the consequences is the loss of tax morale on which the whole system of taxation in free, democratic societies is based.

The cases shown make clear that *not all* interventions from outside via monetary payments or regulations lead to unfortunate consequences: the girl given a bicycle for her general willingness to help with the household chores does not lose her motivation to contribute her share to family life. Similarly, a manager who receives a high salary because he or she does the job well raises, rather than lowers, his or her efforts to run the company. The problems identified are thus complex and eschew any mechanistic treatment; what is needed is an approach taking the underlying psychological intricacies into account.

III   OTHER AREAS ARE AFFECTED

Case 2 involving the boy who, in reaction to being paid each time he mows the family lawn, refuses to do any other household work for free suggests that there is yet another relationship at work. A loss of motivation willingly to cut the lawn spreads over to other familial housework. While such a reaction is awkward within an intact family, such a 'Spill-Over Effect' may have catastrophic consequences in other parts of society. One of the most pressing problems of modern societies is to find sites for collectively desired but locally unwanted installations, such as asylums for the mentally handicapped or hospitals for the physically handicapped and the sick (for instance, for persons infected with AIDS); for prisons, power plants and nuclear refuse repositories, as well as for regional and national roads, railway tracks and air terminals. Until recently, the respective sites could normally be secured as the inhabitants of the respective communes have found it natural to contribute to the 'common good' (as long as they could be confident that the other citizens would also take their share of duties). Today however, the situation is drastically changed, and the principle of NIMBY, that is, 'Not In My BackYard', has taken over. On the basis of a cost–benefit calculation, the inhabitants of a commune refuse to host such a site because they would have to carry most of the cost while the benefit of having the installations accrues to society as a whole. Economists have a ready solution to this problem: offer the commune a monetary compensation for the cost imposed, possibly by using an auction system. However, such a solution has a major disadvantage. The money offer crowds-out the citizens' motivation to do anything for the common good. Moreover, no other commune will be prepared to host such a facility for free in the future. As a consequence, it often becomes impossible to undertake socially beneficial projects. Similarly, unfortunate Spill-Over Effects are to be expected when a commune is *forced* by the central state to accept a locally unwanted installation.

The book's purpose is to analyse these issues in depth, and to put them into a theoretical perspective. It may be helpful to summarize the relationships in question (Table 2.1).

Table 2.1   Classification of external interventions and intrinsic motivation

Outside interferences	Effect on intrinsic motivation		Effects on intrinsic motivation in related areas
	desired (Crowding-In)	undesired (Crowding-Out)	(Spill-Over)
Payment (monetary incentive)			
Command (regulation)			

Table 2.1 distinguishes two types of interferences from outside the person (money payment and command). The effects on intrinsic motivation may be desired in each case – which will be called 'Crowding-In' – or undesired – called 'Crowding-Out'. (The effect may, of course, also be neutral.) Moreover, each type of intervention can produce Spill-Overs on related areas. Hence, six different cases have to be distinguished.

The analysis will be strongly empirically oriented. What matters is not theoretical analysis *per se* but the relevance for economic policy.

Consequently, an effort will be made to adduce as much empirical evidence as is available. Most importantly, the 'Crowding Effects' and the 'Spill-Over Effect' are applied to socially relevant policy areas. Many of the cases only hinted at in this introductory section are discussed in depth in Part II of this book.

SUGGESTED FURTHER READINGS

A large number of examples for Crowding Effects are given in
Deci, Edward L. with Richard Flaste (1995), *Why We Do What We Do. The Dynamics of Personal Autonomy*, New York: Putnam.
The motivational limits of paying to increase effort is discussed with many examples by
Kohn, Alfie (1993), *Punished by Rewards: The Trouble with Gold Stars, Incentive Plans, A's Praise, and Other Bribes*, Boston: Houghton Mifflin.
The consequences for management are discussed in an article
Kohn, Alfie (1993), 'Why Incentive Plans Cannot Work', *Harvard Business Review*, 5 (Sept./Oct.), 54–63.
The 'Not-In-My-BackYard' problem is, for example, treated in
Portney, Kent E. (1991), *Siting Waste Treatment Facilities: The NIMBY Syndrome*, New York: Auburn House.

3. The psychological background

I EXTRINSIC AND INTRINSIC MOTIVATION

The economic model of human behaviour is based on incentives applied from outside the person considered: people change their actions because they are induced to do so by an external intervention (see Becker, 1976; Coleman, 1990; Frey, 1992a). Economic theory thus takes *extrinsic motivation* to be relevant for behaviour.

Economists do not deny that some people are sometimes induced by 'inner feelings', or *intrinsic motivation*, but they do not attach much importance to that factor. One reason is that they do not feel competent to determine what an individual's preferences are. Another is that they are convinced that incentives applied from outside are more important, and that by far the most effective motivator is money. They are fond of proclaiming that 'everything has its price'. A third reason is methodological. Individual preferences are not used to explain human behaviour because such a procedure easily becomes tautological. To 'explain', for instance, that somebody uses her car less by saying that 'she is less fond of driving her car', is just a restatement but does not provide new insights. To attribute behaviour (or a behavioural change) to a particular preference (or preference change) cannot be tested empirically as long as there is no independent observation that the person does indeed like to drive a car less. For that reason, it has become accepted practice to attribute changes in behaviour to independently observable changes in constraints (Stigler and Becker, 1977). In the case of the car driver, such changes in constraint, or in generalized relative prices, may for instance be a rise in car and petrol prices, in insurance premiums, in parking fees, or newly instituted traffic rules and regulations.

Psychologists, on the other hand, emphasize the behavioural motives coming from within the person. Following Deci (1971, p. 105), 'one is said to be intrinsically motivated to perform an activity when one receives no apparent reward except the activity itself'. A psychologist such as Fischhoff (1982) sees intrinsic motivation as the primary behavioural motive of human beings (see also Staw, 1976; Arnold, 1976; or more recently Hirst, 1988; or Scott *et al.*, 1988). Intrinsic motivation is a firmly established concept in psychology (and partly in other social sciences such as sociology); it goes back to DeCharms (1968) and Deci (1975).

The distinction between intrinsic and extrinsic motivation is not clear-cut. Indeed, it can even be claimed that in the last instance, all motivations come from outside. When someone climbs a high mountain, one can always find an extrinsic incentive such as recognition by friends, or when someone spends hours with his play trains one could attribute the expectation that they can, in future, be sold for a high price. On the other hand, recognition and monetary gain are not final goals; what matters after all is the intrinsic satisfaction one derives. It may well be that the precise distinction is important for psychology. On the other hand, for the purpose of explaining economically and socially relevant human behaviour, it suffices that it makes sense to distinguish activities which individuals (mainly) do just because they like them, and others which they (mainly) do because they are induced to do so by monetary payment or by command.[1] In many cases, the two motivations come together. A person may exert great efforts in climbing mountains not just for fun, but also to impress her friends. Someone also collects play trains out of fascination with this toy, but is not averse to selling his collection when the time arrives. Turning to famous persons: why did Emily Dickinson write poetry without any inclination to publish a single line? Why did Goethe seal Faust II for posthumous publication? Why did Cavendish undertake experiments in his private laboratory without any desire to announce his inventions to the public? Why did the mathematician Galois, facing death in a dual the next morning, stay awake all night to write down his major discoveries in higher algebra? (He would certainly have been better off getting a good night's sleep.) (Simonton, 1994, p. 207.)

For our purpose, the distinction between intrinsic and extrinsic motivation is not relevant as such. What is crucial is the systematic relationship between the two. This is the topic to which we now turn.

II   THE HIDDEN COST OF REWARD

A group of social psychologists[2] have identified that under particular conditions monetary (external) rewards undermine intrinsic motivation.

The application of rewards for undertaking an activity thus has indirect negative consequences. For that reason, this effect has been termed 'The Hidden Cost of Reward' (see Lepper and Greene, 1978, who give an account and extensive references). Many laboratory experiments support this motivational effect: 'The evidence for a detrimental effect comes from a wide variety of works in which a large number of subjects and methodological parameters have been varied' (McGraw, 1978, pp. 55–8).

My co-workers Iris Bohnet, Reiner Eichenberger and Felix Oberholzer-Gee and I undertook an experiment at the University of Zurich in autumn 1994 using the framework of the Dictator Game (developed by Kahneman, Knetsch and Thaler, 1986a and b). The purpose was to test the extent to which individuals are prepared to share funds with others, which is a particular kind of intrinsic motivation (altruism). The students (N=14) initially received an endowment of CHF 7.– and in the first treatment condition were asked to pass on at least CHF 2.50 to an anonymous other person. Under these conditions, the median amount given was CHF 3.–. When the same persons thereafter were again endowed with CHF 7.– but without any minimum sharing rule imposed, the median amount allocated to the second person was CHF 1.80. This reduction in the amount shared is especially surprising as a different group of subjects (N=14) who were confronted with the sharing decision without any prior enforcement passed on CHF 3.–. The difference between CHF 3.– (unforced treatment) and CHF 1.80 (forced treatment) is consistent with the Crowding-Out Effect. The same experiment (N=14) was repeated with a mandatory donation of CHF 4.– to be given. In this situation the median amount passed on was CHF 4.–. When the rule was lifted, it dropped to CHF 2.– which is again clearly lower than the CHF 3.– given in the unforced treatment. The experimental result is again consistent with the Crowding-Out Effect: the subjects' altruism of giving to other persons was undermined when they were *forced* to share with another person.

As is perfectly normal in empirically oriented sciences including applied econometrics, such effects are never undisputed. By now a very large number of controlled laboratory experiments have been undertaken to test the relationship between reward and intrinsic motivation. Not surprisingly, the results are not as unequivocal as McGraw claimed in 1978. The reason is that both sides of the relationship can be defined, operationalized and measured in many different ways: what is 'a reward', what is 'intrinsic motivation'? Depending on what definitions and concepts are used, and under what general circumstances the relationship is tested, it is possible to produce almost any result.[3] The usefulness of a psychological effect for socio-economic analysis does not rest on whether it always obtains. Rather, the conditions under which an effect holds must be identified. What also matters is that the examples discussed in Chapter 2, which are based on both personal experiences and circumstantial evidence, can be related to the experimental analysis. As mentioned, the negative relationship between external intervention and intrinsic motivation is relevant even though it exists only under some conditions and, in many cases, is neutral or even positive.

The research on the hidden cost of reward has had immediate consequences for practical applications of psychology. For a considerable number of years patients in old age homes and psychiatric asylums were believed to be motivated to at least partially care for themselves if they were given tokens which they could redeem for various goods at the asylum store. It has, however, turned out that such 'token economy' programmes had limited success and that the high hopes did not materialize (see the surveys by Kazdin and Bootzin, 1972; Kazdin, 1982). The offer of tokens for making the bed, or keeping the room clean, promoted a general attitude that the patients were not responsible for anything *per se*. Only if they received a payment in the form of tokens were they prepared to do any work at all. For the rest of the wide-ranging activities in such asylums, the patients actively transferred the task and responsibility to the staff. As tokens can only be given for a limited number of well-defined tasks (not least because of the transaction costs involved), the increased involvement and participation of the patients proved to be largely futile, so that in most asylums, the token economy systems have either been discontinued or never introduced.

III PSYCHOLOGICAL PROCESSES

The hidden cost of reward may be attributed to three psychological processes:

(a) *Impaired Self-Determination*. When individuals perceive an external intervention to reduce their self-determination, they substitute intrinsic motivation for extrinsic control. Following Rotter (1966), the locus of control has shifted from the inside to the outside of the person affected. The persons concerned no longer feel themselves to be responsible, but rather the person or institution undertaking the interference from outside. As a result,the intrinsic motivation is partly or wholly given up. The account just given of the effect of token systems in asylums is a good case illustrating this transfer of the locus of control.

(b) *Impaired Self-Esteem*. When an intervention from outside carries the notion that the actor's intrinsic motivation is not acknowledged, his or her intrinsic motivation is effectively rejected. The person affected feels that his or her involvement and competence is not appreciated which debases its value. An intrinsically motivated person is denied the chance to display his or her own interest and involvement in an activity when someone else offers a reward, or commands, to undertake it. As a result of impaired self-esteem,[4] individuals reduce effort.

(c) *Impaired Expression Possibility*. A person acting on the basis of his or her intrinsic motivation is deprived of the chance to exhibit this intrinsic motivation to other persons. They exhibit 'altruistic anger' and will in reaction relinquish the inner motivation and behave according to external motives.

These three psychological processes are closely related to each other, and partly overlap. In all cases, intrinsic incentives are substituted by extrinsic incentives.

Individuals who are forced to behave in a specific way by outside intervention, feel overjustified if they maintain their intrinsic motivation ('Overjustification Effect'). This behaviour is perfectly consistent with a rational choice point of view. Individuals reduce the factor that they control themselves, that is, intrinsic motivation, when they are subjected to outside incentives, and it has therefore become unnecessary to be moreover intrinsically motivated; behaviour becomes more strongly extrinsically guided.

IV   CONDITIONS FOR THE CROWDING EFFECT

On the basis of these two psychological processes, the 'hidden cost of reward' may be generalized. The 'hidden cost' not only appears when a monetary reward is offered but also when the intervention is in the form of *regulations*. In both cases of external intervention, an overjustification effect may be produced, and self-esteem may be reduced. It could even be hypothesized that these psychological processes are often more intensive when individuals are confronted with strict commands. After all, with monetary rewards, an individual has a measure of choice. If he or she wants to maintain self-determination, the monetary offer can be rejected. Of course, this creates an opportunity cost amounting to the size of the reward, but experimental research suggests that opportunity cost often has lesser weight than direct cost (which arises when a command is not followed, (see Thaler, 1980)).

The psychological processes identified in the last section also allow us to derive the *psychological conditions* under which the Crowding-Out Effect appears: (1) External interventions *crowd out* intrinsic motivation if the individuals affected perceive them to be *controlling*. In that case, self-determination, self-esteem and the possibility for expression suffer, and the individuals react by reducing their intrinsic motivation in the activity controlled. (2) External interventions *crowd in* intrinsic motivation if the individuals concerned perceive it as *supportive*. In that case, self-esteem is fostered, and individuals feel that they are given more freedom to act, thus enlarging self-determination.

Both conditions are formulated in terms of subjective perception. It is therefore possible that the same intervention is perceived as controlling by one person (thus reducing intrinsic effort), and as supportive by another person (thus raising intrinsic effort). In order to apply these conditions to socio-economic issues going beyond a particular individual, it is necessary to find empirically observable conditions under which these perceptions typically arise. This will be undertaken in the next chapter. Equally important is to go beyond the effect of external interventions on intrinsic motivation and to analyse the effect on behaviour. For that purpose, one needs simultaneously to take into account the (generalized) Price Effect normally considered in economics jointly with the Crowding Effects.

NOTES

1. Joan Robinson used to say that a huge majority of persons recognize an elephant even though they are quite incapable of defining it exactly. We all know how difficult it is to state what a 'chair' is, but in practical life most of us are perfectly competent to use it and to speak about it.
2. Headed by Deci (1971, 1972, 1975, 1987). The work is summarized and extended

in Deci and Ryan (1980, 1985). Extensive surveys are given in Lepper and Greene (1978), Pittman and Heller (1987), and Lane (1991, esp. ch. 19).
3. See, for instance, the surveys and meta-analyses by Wiersma (1992) and Cameron and Pierce (1994) where hundreds of experimental studies are cited, evaluated and compared.
4. Self-esteem is not a category used in economics but is taken to be of central importance for human beings by many scholars outside economics. See, for instance, Rawls (1971, p. 86) who considers self-esteem to be the most valuable of the goods he designates as 'primary'.

SUGGESTED FURTHER READINGS

The research on the hidden cost of reward is summarized in
Deci, Edward L. and Richard M. Ryan (1985), *Intrinsic Motivation and Self-Determination in Human Behavior*, New York: Plenum Press.
Many important contributions are collected in
Lepper, Mark R. and David Greene (eds) (1978), *The Hidden Costs of Rewards: New Perspectives on the Psychology of Human Motivation*, Hillsdale, N.Y.: Erlbaum.
A survey of motivational psychology is given, for instance, in
Weiner, Bernard (1992), *Human Motivation*, New York and London: Sage.
Modern treatises of social psychology are, for example
Hewstone, Miles; Wolfgang Stroebe and Geoffrey M. Stephenson (eds) (1996), *Introduction to Social Psychology. A European Perspective*, Oxford: Blackwell.
Brigham, J.C. (1991), *Social Psychology*, New York: Harper Collins.
The work on 'token economy' has been evaluated by
Kazdin, A.E. (1982), 'The Token Economy: A Decade Later', *Journal of Applied Behavioural Analysis*, **15**, 431–45.

4. Integration into economics

I A RICHER MODEL OF HUMAN BEHAVIOUR

Economics explains the behaviour of individuals by drawing on the (relative) Price Effect. It states that human beings *ceteris paribus* increase an activity whose reward or price, in comparison with other relevant prices, rises.[1] Individuals are thus persuaded to work more and harder when the respective monetary incentive rises. Modern economics, and in particular principal–agent theory (see, for example, Hart and Holmström, 1987; Stiglitz, 1987, 1991; Petersen, 1993) relies on this relationship and therefore argues, for instance, that workers and employees should, as far as at all feasible, be paid according to how they perform.

Psychology is more concerned with motivations coming from the inside of persons. The Crowding-Out Effect shows that external interventions, and in particular monetary rewards, undermine such intrinsic motivations and therewith reduce work effort when the individuals affected feel that their self-determination and self-esteem is impaired. It need not be stressed that our Crowding-Out Effect has nothing to do with crowding-out as discussed in macroeconomics. That increased public investment tends to replace private investment or, more generally, that public outlays tend to drive out private expenditures, is due to the Price Effect and takes place without any change in preferences.

What is now needed is to look at these two countervailing effects in perspective. For that purpose, a simple model is constructed which is able neatly to integrate the Price Effect and the Crowding Effect.

The impact of an external intervention (E) upon behaviour can best be shown in the context of a principal–agent relationship: the principal uses rewards and commands in order to raise the performance (P) of the agent. The agent could be an employee or worker in a firm, but more generally everyone who is given a task to perform.

A (representative) agent performs by considering the benefits B and the cost C entailed. Both increase in performance, that is, $\partial B/\partial P \equiv B_P > 0$ and $\partial C/\partial P \equiv C_P > 0$.

Higher performance has diminishing marginal returns ($B_{PP} < 0$) and is associated with increasing marginal cost ($C_{PP} > 0$). Benefits and cost are also influenced by the principal's external intervention:

$$B = B(P, E); B_P > 0, B_{PP} < 0. \tag{1}$$

$$C = C(P, E); C_P > 0, C_{PP} > 0. \tag{2}$$

A rational agent chooses that level of performance P^* which maximizes net benefits ($B - C$), which yields the first order condition

$$B_P = C_P. \tag{3}$$

An individual thus increases his or her performance until the marginal benefits equal the marginal cost of so doing. The agent's optimal performance P^* is affected when the principal changes the extent of external intervention E. The result is mathematically shown by differentiating the optimality condition for performing (3) with respect to E:

$$B_{PE} + B_{PP} \frac{dP^*}{dE} = C_{PE} + C_{PP} \frac{dP^*}{dE}, \text{ or}$$

$$\frac{dP^*}{dE} = \frac{B_{PE} - C_{PE}}{C_{PP} - B_{PP}} \gtrless 0. \tag{4}$$

Three cases may be distinguished:

(a) Following the standard economic principal–agent theory (for example, Alchian and Demsetz, 1972; Fama and Jensen, 1983), external intervention raises performance by imposing higher marginal cost on shirking or, equivalently, by lowering the marginal cost of performing, $C_{PE} < 0$. This is the Relative Price Effect of external intervention. One could also speak of a disciplining effect which monetary reward or commands impose on an agent. On the other hand, the Crowding-Out Effect is neglected, that is, a change in external intervention does not affect the marginal benefit of performing ($B_{PE} = 0$), as intrinsic motivation is, implicitly, taken to be a constant (or, rather absent). According to orthodox principal–agent theory, an external intervention therefore always raises performance:

$$\mathrm{d}P^*/\mathrm{d}E > 0. \tag{4a}$$

The same outcome holds if external intervention increases intrinsic motivation. In that case, the marginal benefit from performing is raised ($B_{PE} > 0$) and the effect through disciplining the agent is further strengthened by the Crowding-In Effect. In this case, the Price Effect works in the same direction as the Crowding Effect.

(b) In contrast, when external intervention undermines intrinsic motivation the agent's marginal benefit from performing is negatively affected ($B_{PE} < 0$, Crowding-Out Effect). If the disciplining effect does not work ($C_{PE} = 0$), a stronger external intervention reduces the agent's performance level:

$$\mathrm{d}P^*/\mathrm{d}E < 0. \tag{4b}$$

(c) In general, both the Price Effect ($C_{PE} < 0$) and the Crowding-Out Effect ($B_{PE} < 0$) are active, so that external intervention has two opposite effects on the agent's performance. Whether intervening is beneficial from the principal's point of view depends on the relative size of the Price and the Crowding-Out Effects.

How should principals act when confronted with these three possible outcomes? How strongly should they externally intervene in order to make their agents act according to their wishes?

Rational principals seek to maximize their utility or profit U, taking into account how the agents react to their intervention, that is, relationship (4). Profit is raised by higher output X which depends (among others) on the agent's performance, but with decreasing returns:

$$X = X(P); \quad X_P > 0, X_{PP} < 0. \tag{5}$$

External intervention imposes increasing marginal costs K on the principal which are composed of monitoring, and punishing employees not performing adequately:

$$K = K(E); \quad K_E > 0, K_{EE} > 0 \tag{6}$$

Maximizing profit $U = X - K$ requires

$$X_P \frac{dP^*}{dE} = K_E \qquad (7)$$

Equation (7) determines the optimal extent of external intervention E^*. It is reached when the marginal gain equals the marginal cost of intervening. It is again useful to distinguish three cases:

(a) External intervention does not affect the agent's optimal performance level ($dP^*/dE = 0$). The principal should then abstain from changing the rewards or regulations of the agent.

(b) The Price Effect of external intervention dominates the Crowding-Out Effect ($dP^*/dE > 0$) which makes it optimal for the principal to intervene more strongly. The same holds when there is a Crowding-In Effect.

(c) The Crowding-Out Effect outweighs the Price Effect ($dP^*/dE < 0$). This makes rational principals reduce their intervention.

Indeed, intervening above the level E^* now carries a cost in terms of reducing the agent's work effort by crowding-out his work morale.

This simple model indicates that empirical research on the crowding effect does not require the direct measurement of intrinsic preferences.[2] The relationship between extrinsic and intrinsic preferences can, as far as it is relevant for behaviour, be empirically analysed by looking at the behaviour of different actors.

Firstly, the behaviour of the *persons affected* by external intervention (the agents) can be empirically evaluated by the equation $P^* = P(E)$ implied by relationship (4). It reveals how the persons adjust their performance P in reaction to the external intervention E. A negative observed relationship ($dP^*/dE < 0$) indicates that for the external intervention in question the Crowding-Out Effect dominates the Relative Price Effect.

Intrinsic motivation may secondly be inferred by analysing the behaviour of the person or institution (the principal) *administering the external intervention*. Given the marginal cost of intervening, a strong reliance on *external intervention* by a rational actor indicates that intrinsic motivation is little or not at all affected. There might even exist a Crowding-In Effect of intervening. On the other hand, under the same condition, a low level of external intervention suggests that rational principals know that intrinsic motivation is crowded out.

II EPISODES OF CROWDING EFFECTS

The three kinds of effects of external interventions especially via monetary incentives (pricing) on intrinsic motivation have been discussed in quite different strands of literature, and can be related to various historical periods.

Crowding-In Effect

That pricing *improves* intrinsic motivation was the dominant view from the 16th to the 19th century (see Hirschman, 1977; 1982). The underlying idea is that, while passions are uncontrolled and hazardous, pursuing one's material interests raises moral standards and the incentive to work hard for its own sake. The clearest exponent of this idea of 'doux commerce' is Montesquieu who, in his *De l'esprit des lois* (1749, vol. XX) states as a matter-of-fact that 'commerce ... polishes and softens ways of behavior as we can see every day'. The conventional wisdom in this period, shared by diverse thinkers such as Condorcet (1795) or Kant (1795), was that pricing not only leads to higher productivity than alternative allocation mechanisms such as planning, but also 'would generate as by-product, or external economy, a more "polished" human type ... more honest, reliable, orderly, and disciplined, as well as more friendly and helpful' (Hirschman, 1982, p. 1465). According to Durkheim (1893/1964), the division of labour which results from the application of pricing and the market also makes people more dependent on each other, increases ties among people and makes them act more productively.

A positive effect of pricing on intrinsic motivation is also posited by several present-day psychological theories. According to equity theory (Adams, 1963; Walster *et al.*, 1977), individuals attempt to make their ratios of outcomes to inputs (in particular their work effort) equivalent to the corresponding ratios of other people. When feeling overpaid, for example, individuals tend to reduce the inequity by doing a better-than-average job. The equity literature therefore predicts and empirically shows that higher pay tends to result in higher productivity (for evidence, see for example Andrews, 1967; Lawler and O'Gara, 1967). Developmental psychologists who study the emergence of motivations in children have also collected evidence that external rewards create and enhance intrinsic motivation (for example Aronfreed, 1968).

Crowding-Neutral Effect

According to standard (neo-classical) economics, monetary rewards do not affect intrinsic motivation. This view is shared by Adam Smith (see Hirschman, 1977, pp. 93–106) as well as by some psychologists. Thus, Scott *et al.* (1988, p. 425) find that 'there is little reason to believe that the design and implementation of a more effective extrinsic reinforcement schedule will destroy one's pride in one's work, the intrinsic worth of meaningfulness of the job, or one's predilection to perform it'.

Crowding-Out Effect

In his book *The Social Limits of Growth*, which had a great influence on the social sciences outside economics, Hirsch (1976) argues that pricing debases moral values such as 'truth, trust, acceptance, restraint, obligation' (p. 143) and tends to reduce the intrinsic motivation to perform. The market destroys its own ethical basis through the 'commercialization effect'. Similar views have been put forward by such diverse scholars as Weber (1920–21), Schumpeter (1942), Bell (1976), and the New Left such as Horkheimer (1952) or Marcuse (1965) (see, more extensively, Hirschman, 1977; 1982). Lawyers (such as Michelman, 1967) and philosophers (such as Singer, 1973) have expressed concern about 'demoralization cost'.

Some modern economists have also remarked that the use of prices may crowd out people's intrinsic motivation (see Sen, 1982; 1987), but they have done so incoherently and without being aware of the psychological literature (exceptions are Maital, 1988, and Schlicht, 1990, p. 361). One such economist is Arrow (1970; 1972) who stresses the importance of maintaining the ethical bases of human action against purely rationalist pricing.

III CONDITIONS FOR CROWDING-OUT

The crucial question of when an external intervention affects individuals' intrinsic motivation negatively, and when positively or not at all, has been considered in Chapter 3 at the psychological level. It has been identified that when such intervention is perceived to be *controlling* by the individuals affected, the reduced self-determination and self-esteem provokes a decrease in intrinsic motivation and we observe crowding-out. In contrast, when the external intervention is perceived to be *supportive*, intrinsic motivation is bolstered and we observe crowding-in.

We now look at the *conditions* that determine whether an outside intervention is considered controlling or supportive. It is analysed how external interventions affect the perceived locus of control and self-determination, as well as perceived self-esteem of the person affected. Psychological research in this area is much concerned with the individual reactions based on personality characteristics; economics on the other hand is interested in knowing which outcome is more likely under what circumstances. When and how should rewards and regulations be applied in order to raise performance? This question is policy-oriented; in particular, the goal is to know which among the many possible institutions should be chosen in order to obtain a particular result (Comparative Analysis of Institutions). The empirical evidence available is restricted in this respect because the laboratory and field experiments undertaken in psychology are not designed to answer this kind of questions. It is therefore necessary theoretically to derive propositions which are in principle amenable to empirical testing. The propositions derived are illustrated where suitable, and available empirical evidence is mentioned.

The first two conditions refer to the amount of intrinsic motivation agents typically exhibit in a situation. The basic idea is that there are situations in which intrinsic motivation is central, and in which therefore an external intervention perceived to be controlling has a strong Crowding-Out Effect. If, in contrast, intrinsic motivation influences behaviour little or not at all, there can be no Crowding-Out Effect.

1 Personal relationships

The persons subject to external intervention may, at the one extreme, be unknown to each other and act anonymously, or, at the other extreme, be friends, family members or lovers. The degree of 'social embeddedness' (Granovetter, 1985), 'cojointness' (Coleman, 1990) or feelings of solidarity (for instance, Lindenberg, 1988) and reciprocity among actors systematically influence crowding.

Proposition 1   The more personal the relationship between principal and agent, the more important is intrinsic motivation. An external intervention disrupts this equilibrium and shifts the locus of control from intrinsic to extrinsic motivation. A Crowding-Out Effect is to be expected.

In industrial relations theory, a personalized or reciprocal relationship between principal and agent has been observed to lead to a 'psychological contract' whose violation tends to reduce work effort and performance. This interpretation is supported by a great deal of empirical evidence (see, for example, Ribeaux and Poppleton, 1978; Beer *et al.*, 1984). Unclearly defined values of the goods and services to be traded are yet another cause for crowding-out. Actors seek to interpret and understand the ambiguity by taking up personal contacts. This aspect is of particular importance, for example, in the arts where values are often undetermined and are established through interchanges and discussions among the persons involved (see, for a similar argument, Klamer 1995).

Institutionally, the degree of embeddedness is reflected by decision-making systems. In perfect competition or in the pure price system, the relationship between the individuals is solely guided by the price, and there is anonymity between the partners. As Smith (1776, quoted after 1979, pp. 232–3) clearly stated: 'Social atomization is prerequisite to perfect competition'. Hence, there is no place for intrinsic motivation and no crowding out can take place. Thus, orthodox economics, as long as it is only concerned with pure market interactions, does not need to consider any effect of relative prices or monetary rewards on (intrinsic) preferences. This condition is, for example, fulfilled when goods are bought in a supermarket; the customer does not to take the supplier's intrinsic motivation into account. To focus solely on the Price Effect of external interventions is in this case warranted.

As soon as one moves outside the pure price system, personal interactions become important. This is obvious for decision-making systems centred on bargaining where the actors necessarily enter into social interactions. Intrinsic motivation plays a role, and often a considerable one; as a consequence, external interventions may crowd-out intrinsic motivation. Within firms, the intensity of the personal relationship between the principals and the agents strongly depends on the form of *supervision* (an aspect which will be extensively discussed in Chapter 10).

Another institutional aspect refers to the *size* of the decision-making unit. The behaviour in an extended family tends to be different from a nuclear family because in the latter intrinsic motivation in the form of altruism is more important and family members are careful not to crowd it out. Thus, monetary rewards are likely to be observed more often, and to a larger extent, among members of an extended family as opposed to a nuclear one. The same can be expected to hold in large compared with small groups. Some organizations such as churches or clubs make a determined effort to establish the atmosphere of a family.

As has been empirically shown (for example, Bonacich, 1986), the more formally the contributions of members to common activities are regulated, the more solidarity between the church members loses importance, and the less the voluntary contributions in terms of work and money are in the long run. At the governmental level, rewards and commands are hypothesized to play a more prominent role in large, unitary states than in small, decentralized jurisdictions.

2 Type of activity
The task or job at hand is perceived to be of different intrinsic interest by the agents, which implies different reactions to external interventions.

Proposition 2   The more interesting a task is for the agents, the higher their intrinsic motivation to perform well, and the more an external intervention diminishes perceived self-determination and self-evaluation, and therewith the intrinsic motivation.

This proposition is supported by much evidence from psychologists in carefully controlled laboratory experiments (see, for example, the surveys by McGraw, 1978 and Lane, 1991). 'Task-contingent rewards impair performance on interesting (complex or conceptual) tasks but they improve performance on dull, repetitive tasks' (Deci and Ryan, 1985, p. 84). The same results have been found for regulations.

Institutionally, it is not easy to indicate *a priori* which tasks and jobs are 'interesting' and which are 'dull', because the evaluation may vary considerably between individuals. However, it seems fair to state that liberal professions such as lawyers, architects, doctors or artists, as well as academics tend to consider their jobs more intrinsically interesting than less educated employees. Following Proposition 2, one would expect that in the liberal professions, *ceteris paribus*, less external intervention is used than in other occupations. This proposition has indeed been supported by much empirical evidence collected in particular by supervision theory (for example, Donaldson, 1980; Reber and van Gilder, 1982).

The following five conditions refer more directly to whether an outside intervention is perceived to be controlling or supportive.

3 Participation
The formal and informal possibilities for agents to participate in the principals' decision process vary widely. In some institutions mainly

commands are used, while in other institutions there is extensive discussion and co-determination.

Proposition 3 The more extensive the agents' participation possibilities are, the more an external intervention shifts the locus of control outwards, thus crowding out intrinsic motivation.

Although it has not necessarily been formulated in these terms, this proposition lies at the heart of the arguments for co-determination.

Institutionally, one may distinguish between *firms* that rely on workers' participation and others which rely on hierarchical commands. With respect to formal as well as informal co-determination, there exist neat differences between countries as well. According to Proposition 3, one expects less intensive external interventions in the latter than in the former type of firm. Among much other evidence in favour of this result, a comparison between Japanese firms relying more on consensus and collaboration of all employees, and American firms relying more on hierarchical decision-making, supports our conclusions (see Aoki, 1990).

At the governmental level, even within one country, there exist different constitutional possibilities for citizens to participate in political decision-making. A case in point is Switzerland, where some cantons have extensive possibilities for direct participation (that is, initiatives and referenda on virtually all issues), while others grant these possibilities only for special issues and under specific conditions. Other cantons rely on the institutions of representative democracy. It may be hypothesized that under cantonal constitutions allowing more direct participation, citizens are more strongly committed. Their political loyalty is more developed and they tend to have a higher tax morale than representative communes. An econometric study supporting this proposition will be presented in Chapter 6.

4 Uniformity
At one extreme, all the agents are treated the same by the principal; at the other extreme, the principal makes a conscious effort to distinguish the rewards or commands according to the agents' presumed level of intrinsic motivation.

Proposition 4 The more uniform the external intervention, the more negatively are those agents affected who have above-average intrinsic motivation. They feel that their competence and involvement are not recognized by the principal and therefore adjust their intrinsic motivation downwards.

An example for this reaction is provided by Case 3 in Chapter 2. The more engaged professors feel unjustly treated by a uniform intervention. As a result, the locus of control shifts from intrinsic to extrinsic motivation, and they reduce their teaching to the minimum number of hours required.

Institutionally, the government administration which is bound by general rules tends to intervene more uniformly than the 'generalization principle' of private institutions. In particular, the government has to obey a general salary scale and cannot vary it according to the intrinsic motivation and performance of an employee. This aspect will be taken up again in Chapter 10.

On the other hand, private institutions typically make a greater effort to distinguish between agents of high and low intrinsic motivation. At private universities, for instance, professors are required to document their research achievements (publications, citations) to the administration. This procedure gives the most prolific and successful researchers a chance to show their competence, raising their intrinsic academic motivation further. At universities run by a central governmental institution – the typical case in Europe – the administration exhibits little or no interest in an academic's performance, so that his or her intrinsic motivation is unaffected (or diminishes over time). The higher intrinsic interest in research, coupled with higher external rewards, is one of the features most often remarked upon by European scholars visiting the United States.

5   Type of intervention: reward versus command

In standard economics, rewards and commands are not differentiated. In both cases, deviating from the principal's desires entails costs. In the case of rewards, the agents suffer the opportunity cost of not receiving the maximum reward; in the case of commands, a deviation is met by punishment. However, with rewards, the agents feel that they have a certain amount of freedom in their intensity of responding. Therefore they perceive rewards as less restrictive to their self-determination than commands, which are felt to intrude directly into the agents' realms of self-determination.

Proposition 5 External interventions via rewards crowd out intrinsic motivation less than regulations used for the same purpose.

This proposition is of immediate institutional relevance. An important case is environmental policy which will be extensively treated in Chapter 7. Economists strongly champion the use of pricing instruments (effluent charges or taxes, tradable licences) because they give individuals and firms incentives to act in an environmentally-friendly way. The 'control and command' approach, on the other hand, is rejected because it does not promote any incentives to safeguard the environment in the long run. According to our proposition, there is an additional advantage of using price incentives over pure commands: the intrinsic motivation to protect nature, or environmental morale, is less damaged.

6 Contingency of rewards on performance

When agents are rewarded only in so far as they exactly perform according to the principals' wishes, their locus of control is shifted outward, and intrinsic is substituted by extrinsic motivation.

Proposition 6 The more closely a reward is contingent on the performance desired by the principal, the more is intrinsic motivation crowded out.

This proposition is supported by many laboratory experiments undertaken by psychologists. Deci and Ryan (1985, p. 81) summarize the result as follows: '... contingent rewards ... tend to decrease intrinsic motivation', and more specifically: 'Competitively contingent rewards are the most controlling, performance-contingent less so, and task-contingent even less than performance-contingent'. The extent to which an agent perceives a reward as being 'contingent' depends on the perceived cause of the reward, the type of reward and the regularity of rewards.

The institutional differences existing between the price system and the administrative system are closely related to various aspects of reward contingency. A monetary reward received through the functioning of the market constitutes a case where the reward depends on performance; in a perfectly competitive market the reward (wage rate) depends exactly on the marginal product performed. The price system therefore tends to substitute intrinsic by extrinsic motivation due to a perceived shift in the locus of control. Moreover, instead of being perceived as a control instrument, a market reward may also indicate competence and then tends to raise intrinsic motivation. Within the bureaucracy of a firm or other organization, the effect of reward contingency depends very much on the context and the way rewards are being applied. These aspects will be more fully discussed in Chapter 9.

7 Hard vs soft regulation

Hard regulation involves enforceable commands including convincing threats of punishment of non-compliance. Soft regulation comprises non-enforceable directives implemented by agreement and without threats of punishment. As hard regulations seek to change behaviour by involuntary means, they shift the locus of control outwards, and favour crowding-out. Soft regulations, in contrast, are unlikely to reduce self-determination, and do not negatively affect the agents' self-esteem. They are therefore maintaining intrinsic motivation, and may even bolster it.

Proposition 7   Hard regulations crowd-out intrinsic motivation, soft regulations tend to leave it unaffected and may even crowd it in.

The distinction between hard and soft regulations has been noted by various scholars. The adversarial system of regulations with respect to environmental and health and safety standards employed in the United States is an example of hard regulation. It has shown to lead to Crowding-Out Effects (see Kelman, 1981; Bardach and Kagan, 1982). In Scandinavian countries, as well as in the Netherlands, the United Kingdom and Switzerland the principle of soft regulation based on a degree of voluntary cooperation is used. As a consequence, the regulated parties (agents) are prepared to go even beyond what is strictly required by law. Other cases of soft regulations are the various international agreements to protect the cultural heritage (for instance by UNESCO). They are not enforceable but are manifestations for the desirability of protective behaviour and therewith support the intrinsic motivation to safeguard the cultural heritage.

8 Message implied by the external intervention

A reward or regulation, respectively, may carry quite a different information which significantly affects the way people perceive them.

Proposition 8 The more strongly an external intervention implies an acknowledgement of the agent's intrinsic motivation, the more strongly it fosters intrinsic motivation.

The perfect market or pure price system entails no moral connotation. A person or firm is completely free to act within the confines of the price set. In so far as the price-external social costs are internalized by Pareto-optimal prices or charges, there is nothing to disapprove of morally. Accordingly, Friedman (1970) argues that the only business of business is to make profit. Actors who partially act according to their moral convictions are often ridiculed.

Once it is taken into account that intrinsic motivation may depend on external intervention, even profit maximizers have to take moral aspects into account. Consider the case of illegal acts. Proponents of the economics of crime (Becker 1976; McKenzie and Tullock, 1975) would argue that in so far as *all* costs imposed by crime were paid, the criminal act should not be morally condemned. To behave legally or illegally would solely be a matter of calculating benefits and costs (but anyone who does not voluntarily agree with the price offered would then be subject to a crime). Most non-economists and also many economists would vehemently oppose such a proposition, not least because they feel that moral barriers against crime are important and necessary since it is impossible to adequately monitor people by applying the appropriate prices. The argument proposed in the economics of crime reaches its extremes when it comes to murder. Should a killer simply be able to pay the appropriate price (which would include compensation to the victim's family) but otherwise go unharmed? The issue is not simply that the appropriate price cannot be administered but that the use of money undermines the moral value of life. Potential murderers have fewer moral qualms to kill. This Crowding-Out Effect leads to socially destructive consequences in the long run.

NOTES

1. This is the pure Relative Price Effect. The income effect may work into the opposite direction but economists have no theory of the direction in which the income effect works; it is just as it is. The Price Effect not only applies to the supply but also to the demand side. A rise in the relative price of a good or activity reduces its demand (again keeping income constant). The successes of the 'economic approach to human behaviour' (Becker, 1976) or of 'economic imperialism' (Stigler, 1984;

Hirshleifer, 1985) are due to the skilful application of the Price Effect. Alchian (1977, p. 179) speaks of 'the simplest and most fundamental postulates and theorems of economics ... The first theorem says individuals act so as to further their own interest ... The second fundamental theorem of economics says the lower the relative price of any good or source of satisfaction the more will be purchased. These are called the first and second fundamental theorems of economics to suggest that their power is comparable to that of the first and second fundamental theorems of physics'. In the same vein Coase (1978, p. 34) states that 'An economist will not debate whether increased punishment [i.e. a higher price or cost, BSF] will reduce a crime; he will merely try to answer the question, by how much'.

2. This is analogous to standard economic theory where the demand for a good depends on marginal utility but empirical (econometric) analyses of demand do not require the direct measurement of a utility function.

SUGGESTED FURTHER READINGS

A short introduction to the Price Effect and its use in the context of the economic model of human behaviour is given by
Hirshleifer, Jack (1985), 'The Expanding Domain of Economics', *American Economic Review*, **75** (Dec), 53–68.
The fundamental contribution is
Becker, Gary S. (1976), *The Economic Approach to Human Behavior*, Chicago: Chicago University Press.
The use of rational choice analysis in sociology has been championed by
Coleman, James S. (1990), *Foundation of Social Theory*, Cambridge, Mass.: Belknap Press of Harvard University.
The basic features of principal–agent theory are presented in
Milgrom, Paul and John Roberts (1992), *Economics, Organization and Management*, Englewood Cliffs: Prentice Hall.
More advanced aspects are treated in
Holmström, Bengt and Paul Milgrom (1991), 'Multi-Task Principal Agent Analyses', *Journal of Law, Economics and Organization*, **7**, 24–52.
The role of Crowding-Out and Crowding-In Effects in history is documented by
Hirschman, Albert O. (1982), 'Rival Interpretations of Market Society: Civilizing, Destructive or Feeble?', *Journal of Economic Literature*, **20**, 1463–84.

5. Motivational Spill-Over Effect

It might be argued that the Crowding Effect discussed so far is of limited importance because a shift in intrinsic motivation can be compensated as long as the Price Effect dominates the Crowding-Out Effect over some range of application of external intervention. This point is certainly reached when the intrinsic motivation initially existing has been completely crowded out. Once this has taken place, external interventions cannot cause any further harm on intrinsic motivation by definition. Provided the Price Effect works, the negative effect on behaviour induced may be compensated by the application of the 'normal' economic instruments. In the case of environmental policy, for example, the reduction in environmental morale induced by a monetary intervention can be made up by a more intensive use of pricing or regulatory instruments. However, such a compensation is either unfeasible or ineffective when the application of external interventions does not only crowd out intrinsic motivation in the specific area, but *spreads beyond*.

The area in which an external intervention is applied need not be the same as the one where intrinsic motivation is affected. If the area covered by a specific type of intrinsic preference is larger than the area influenced by a reward or command, the crowding out of intrinsic motivation 'spills over'. (Empirical evidence on the 'Spill-Over Effect' is given in Kahn and Schooler, 1983 and Warr, 1987, p. 72–6). An example is provided by Case 2 of Chapter 2. The boy paid for mowing the lawn has not only less intrinsic motivation to do that work, but is also unwilling to do any *other* housework for free. The area of control by reward is smaller (it only covers lawn mowing), while intrinsic motivation extends over all housework. If this applies, intervening externally has higher costs than if the Spill-Over Effect did not exist; it is then advisable to apply external intervention less intensively, or not at all.

A spill-over is more likely to obtain, the more costly an agent finds it to differentiate his or her motivation according to a particular area. There are only a few hints on this process in the literature and they are never connected with the Crowding Effect. According to Frank (1988,

p. 162), neurological research suggests that the modular construction of our brains limits the power to differentiate between varying circumstances, in our case to whether external interventions are applicable in an area. In psychology, this is known as the 'spread effect' (Thorndike, 1933). Economist Jensen (1992) deals with 'reputational spill-overs'. Williamson (1975, pp. 37 and 256; 1993), using a similar concept of 'attitudinal spill-over', warns that technical separability (in our case whether prices are applied or not) does not imply attitudinal separability (what area intrinsic motivation refers to), but he does not explore the issue further. Akerlof (1989, p. 93) notes that 'sociologists and anthropologists have asserted that problems of thought concerning one area are duplicated in other seemingly unrelated areas'. Sugden (1989) argues that norms can be spread by analogy. If an analogy can be drawn between an area in which a norm holds and another area in which it does not yet hold, its validity can expand to the latter area as well.

The Spill-Over Effect may not only relate to areas but also to *people* and over *time*. Individuals may reduce their own intrinsic motivation when someone else's intrinsic motivation has been crowded out. This effect is most likely to happen in a closed group, as well as among friends and relatives. Changes in intrinsic motivation typically spill over to subsequent time periods which are not directly affected by an external intervention. Work motivation, for example, which has been crowded out by a controlling intervention is likely to be on that lower level for extended future periods even if the destructive effect is no longer in force.

The following conjectures about the determinants of the extent of motivation spill-overs, partly supported by empirical and circumstantial evidence, may be advanced. The spill-over is expected to be the larger:

(a)   the more similar the areas in question are perceived to be with respect to *material content*. An example is intrinsic motivation with respect to the preservation of the environment which pertains to all areas of nature, irrespective of whether there is an external intervention or not. The idea that similarity or perceived equality of content favours positive spill-overs is supported by experiments undertaken by social psychologists (see Deci, 1972; 1975, p. 157).

(b)   The more similar the *people* are who act in an area with or without external intervention. It has, for example, been argued that undermining tax morale spills over to the rest of the society: '... tax non-compliance may be creating a nation where citizens' disrespect for tax laws will expand disrespect for other laws' (Graetz *et al.*, 1986, p. 2). This Spill-Over Effect is the larger the more one's friends, relatives or neighbours (that is, similar people as oneself) cheat on taxes (see Cialdini, 1989, p. 215)

(c) The stronger the personal interaction in the various areas is. This relationship has been (indirectly) supported in an experiment undertaken at the University of Zurich (see Frey and Bohnet, 1996). One person (the allocator) was given a sum of money (CHF 7.–) and he was told that he was free to give all, nothing, or any amount to two other persons, the recipients (this is an extended Dictator Game). When the recipients were unknown to the allocator (anonymity), each one was given 14 per cent of the sum received. If *one* of the two recipients was identified to the allocator, she receives almost twice as much than under anonymity, namely 24 per cent. What matters in our context is, however, that the non-identified (that is, anonymous) second recipient also receives more than before, namely 17 per cent, which can be interpreted as a Spill-Over Effect. A Spill-Over Effect of similar magnitude could be observed when the allocator could talk with *one* of the two recipients. Again, the more strongly activated norm of fair division is transferred to another person.

(d) The more similar the *processes* that are used in the two sectors. The borders between the areas become blurred, raising the cost of distinction (see Deci, 1972, for experimental evidence).

(e) The stronger the social, religious and ideological *norms, conventions and customs* urging individuals to apply the same intrinsic motivation or morale in all spheres of life. '... Conventions may spread by analogy from one context to another. If it is a matter of common knowledge that a particular convention is followed in one situation, then that convention acquires prominence for other, analogous situations' (Sugden, 1989, p. 93). Christianity and many other religions, for example, do not differentiate between the commandments to be obeyed in the pricing and non-pricing sectors.

A principal maximizing the performance of the agents sets the appropriate financial rewards, but now takes into account the *indirect* effect of external interventions on intrinsic motivation in other areas. But the principal only does so if his or her interests are affected. (i) In the case of *motivation crowding-in and spillovers*, the optimal financial reward is higher than it would be without the Spill-Over Effect. The principals use monetary rewards more extensively to increase agents' performance if they are aware that the agents' intrinsic motivation is at the same time bolstered and spills over to areas where they cannot intervene. (ii) A more interesting case obtains when pricing *crowds out intrinsic motivation* and intrinsic motivation in other areas follows suit. If the direct and indirect motivational effect from the very beginning dominates the Price Effect, rational principals optimally refrain from intervening at all. They recognize that while an increase in, for instance, financial rewards motivates the agents to improve their performance, the destructive effects of pricing on intrinsic motivation, and its spill-over into areas in which pricing is not applied, may be stronger. Under these circumstances, intervening has counterproductive effects, and principals do better to rely on the intrinsic motivation of the agents.

A particularly important instance in which such a counterproductive outcome is relevant refers to political decisions. By constitutional design, the behaviour of individuals in democracies is not guided by the application of price incentives, but is importantly based on intrinsic motivation in the form of civic virtues. This is especially so where low-cost decisions such as voting are involved. (For the concept of low-cost decision making see Kirchgässner and Pommerehne, 1993.) If agents' intrinsic motivation is impaired by external interventions, and this effect moreover spills over into the political arena, then the agents' incentive to politically support the aims desired by the principal decreases (for empirical evidence see Hawkins and Thomas, 1984, p. 55; Kagan and Scholz, 1984, pp. 73–4). Rational principals in that case are more reluctant to use monetary rewards or commands in the economic area when they are aware that the induced damage to intrinsic motivation has negative repercussions on the political sphere.

The situation is quite different when the Spill-Over Effect takes place but the principal's interests are not affected by the fall in intrinsic motivation induced by his or her intervention. The persons responsible tend to discount the future especially if they are appointed for a limited period of time. Thus bureaux are never in charge of all NIMBY-type projects, but only for a particular type, for example, for finding a site for a nuclear waste repository, or for a hospital for mentally disadvantaged persons. Those responsible for one type are little concerned whether the chance of finding a site for another type of NIMBY-project is adversely affected. This condition often exists when a site for a socially beneficent but locally undesired project or installation is sought. All communities tend to act according to the NIMBY-principle. The public bureau in charge of finding a site (the principal) is little or not at all concerned that offering a monetary compensation may result in no other commune being prepared to accept such a project. Even if the bureau concerned does not only have to find one particular site but is also responsible for finding future sites, a negative externality may occur: in that case a negative external effect is produced. If the citizens generally lose the intrinsic motivation to support the 'common good' and to accept any such site, it becomes increasingly difficult to undertake socially desirable projects with locally concentrated cost. In this case, the Spill-Over Effect produces a negative externality which the principals do not take into account in their calculus. The overall allocation of resources is thereby worsened.

SUGGESTED FURTHER READINGS

The Spill-Over Effect has so far not been analysed in the context of Crowding Effects. Similar concepts have, however, been used for other purposes, for instance by

Williamson, Oliver E. (1993), 'Calculativeness, Trust and Economic Organization', *Journal of Law and Economics*, **36** (April), 453–86.

Frank, Robert H. (1988), *Passions Within Reason. The Strategic Role of Emotions*, New York: Norton.

Akerlof, George A. (1989), 'The Economics of Illusion', *Economics and Politics*, **1**, 1–15.

The psychological background is discussed in

Cialdini, Robert B. (1989), 'Social Motivations to Comply: Norms, Values and Principles', in Jeffrey A. Roth and John T. Scholz (eds), *Tax Compliance*, **2**, Philadelphia: University of Pennsylvania Press, 200–227.

Hatfield, Elaine, John T. Cacioppo and Richard L. Rapson (1994), *Emotional Contagion*, Cambridge: Cambridge University Press.

Relevant also is

Sugden, Robert (1989), 'Spontaneous Order', *Journal of Economic Perspectives*, **3** (Fall), 85–97.

Empirical evidence on a Spill-Over Effect between work and leisure is collected in

Warr, Peter (1987), *Work, Unemployment, and Mental Health*, Oxford: Clarendon Press.

PART II
Applications

6. A strict or lenient constitution?

I   DIVERGENT VIEWS

A prevalent view among economists is that citizens, if given the opportunity, act as knaves or crooks. (See in particular Brennan and Buchanan, 1983.) They conclude that a constitution should be designed to limit the extent of exploitative behaviour. The same view has been shared by David Hume (1711–76) and John Stuart Mill (1806–73).

> In contriving any system of government, and fixing the several checks and controls of the constitution, every man ought to be supposed a knave, and to have no other end, in all his actions, than private interest. (David Hume, 'Of Independency of Parliament', *Essays. Moral, Political, and Literary*, vol. 1, Oxford: Oxford University Press, [1742] 1963, pp. 117–18)

> The very principle of constitutional government requires it to be assumed that political power will be abused to promote the particular purposes of the holder, not because it always is so, but because such is the natural tendency of things to guard against which is the especial use of free institutions. (John Stuart Mill, 'Considerations on Representative Government', *Essays on Politics and Society*, vol. 19 of the *Collected Works*, London: Forum Books [1861] 1951, p. 505)

Brennan and Buchanan offer two distinct propositions: (i) people are knaves if not constrained; (ii) a realistic model of (average) human behaviour is not a reasonable basis for normative institutional design because the harm caused by deviations away from the ideal is disproportionally large (convexity assumption). Rather, the worst-case scenario must be considered and society's laws must be so strict that they prevent such malevolent behaviour.

These propositions form the basis of constitutional economics (see Mueller, 1995; Buchanan, 1987). This view has not gone unchallenged.[1] Musgrave (1981) rejects this negative view of human beings, and many authors (for instance, recently Cooter, 1984, 1994; Kelman, 1987; Dryzek, 1992; Mansbridge, 1994) point out that public spiritedness or civic virtues exist in many polities. They argue that public virtue should be actively fostered. This contrasts with Robertson's (1956) insistence of 'economizing on love', a notion generally shared among economists (see also Brennan and Hamlin, 1995). Fostering public virtue is not inconsistent with self-interest (see Kelman, 1969, p. 283): citizens may accord legitimacy to the political system, and therefore be prepared to observe its rules because of long-term rather than short-term self-interest. According to Tyler (1990, p. 20) '... it has been widely suggested [in the social science literature, BSF] that in democratic societies the legal system cannot function if it can influence people only by manipulating rewards and costs' (see also Easton, 1975; Parsons, 1967 or Sarat, 1975).

This chapter does not take issue with the two Brennan–Buchanan propositions as such, but wants to draw attention to a crucial aspect disregarded by them: a constitution designed for knaves tends to drive out civic virtues. As a result, the constitution is less observed. The effort to guard the constitution against exploitation may thus lead to a perverse result. Although a constitution, and more generally public laws and regulations, must check against knaves, it should also support civic virtues. The general spirit of the law, including specific rules, should acknowledge the citizens' basic good will and should support public spiritedness while still preventing exploitation by free riders.

Many scholars outside economics are, however, seriously concerned with the general tendency that government may drive out civic virtues. Thus Goodin (1980) recognizes that governments using both material and moral incentives to the same end, destroy the 'purity and seriousness of moral incentives' while individuals will simply remove those moral considerations from their decision calculus. According to Elster (1989, p. 180) it follows that: 'If people feel that they are taken advantage of, why should they not rip off the system in return? By contrast, political systems that leave more decisions to the individual can both economize on information and generate more trust'.

Our knowledge of the conditions under which civic virtues and other moral motivations are undermined has much progressed recently. Crowding-Out Theory derived from social psychology and applied to economics is more differentiated than the hunch expressed by the above authors.

II CONSTITUTIONAL DESIGN

Crowding Theory can be applied to how constitutional and other legal rules affect the individual citizens. Civic virtue is bolstered if the public laws convey the notion that citizens are trusted (see Proposition 8 in Chapter 4). Such trust is reflected in extensive rights and participation possibilities (see Proposition 3 in Chapter 4). Citizens are given the freedom to act on their own with respect to economic affairs, the freedom to express themselves and to demonstrate and strike if they feel dissatisfied with particular government decisions, and most importantly, to take important political decisions by themselves via referenda and initiatives. The basic notion enshrined in the constitution that citizens are on average, and in general, reasonable human beings thus generates a Crowding-In Effect of civic virtue.

In contrast, a constitution which implies a fundamental distrust in its citizens and seeks to discipline them tends to crowd out civic virtue and undermines the support which citizens are prepared to exert towards the basic law. This distrust towards the citizens shows itself in various ways. Most broadly, it consists in curtailing institutions of direct democracy because the 'classe politique' feels that citizens are unable to take reasoned political decisions. A case in point is the constitution (Grundgesetz) of the Federal Republic of Germany which almost completely excludes forms of direct democracy (referenda, initiatives) because well-meaning politicians in the Constitutional Assembly (wrongly) argued that these institutions brought Hitler to power. A sign of distrust towards the citizens is also embedded in the constitution when government is given much supervisory power, and when little room is left to the individuals to act on their own. In that case controls by bureaucracy and police are extensive, and a citizen is taken not to be trustworthy. The burden of proof to have acted correctly lies with the individual citizen while the public authority is considered to be correct *a priori*.

An important case is provided by the fundamental attitude enshrined in tax laws. In some countries it is assumed that all citizens want to cheat on taxes, and they therefore have to prove that they have paid all what they legally owe. In other countries it is assumed that the citizens are prepared to pay their 'fair share', and the tax administration has to prove that this is not the case. Even if it suspects that not all taxable income has been declared, it tends to attribute it to an error on the taxpayer's side (which indeed is often the case, see Alm, Jackson and McKee, 1992), rather than an attempt purposely to cheat on taxes.

The effects of a distrustful constitution show up in various ways. The citizens are dissatisfied with the political system and respond by breaking the constitution and its laws whenever they expect to do so at low cost. The interactions between individuals and the government is characterized by high transaction costs and low productivity. As the political system functions badly, general cynicism tends to take over. Such a development has occurred in many communist countries and still exists in totalitarian systems (see Vogel, 1965 and Gross, 1982). Another consequence is the refusal to accept projects in the general interest by the local citizens who have to carry major costs, that is, the already mentioned NIMBY-reaction. Another important reaction to distrustful public laws is tax evasion, or the effort to minimize one's tax burden by illegitimate or illegal action.

The mistrust embedded in the constitution has so far been interpreted to be directed against the citizens. This corresponds to the statement reproduced by David Hume who explicitly says '... every man ought to be supposed to be a knave ...'. John Stuart Mill's statement is slightly different as he speaks of '... political power will be abused ...' which suggests that the checks have to be directed against (professional) politicians. This is also the main thrust of the argument for a strict constitution as advanced by Brennan and Buchanan (1983, 1985). It is of special importance because 'bad' politicians can impose great harm on others, while 'bad' citizens can do so much less; normally they can only cheat for their own advantage, particularly on taxes. The question is whether it is possible to design a constitution which enshrines trust towards normal citizens (in order to safeguard their civic virtue), and at the same time mistrusts politicians (in order to prevent them exploiting the ordinary citizens). In so far as the ordinary citizens are given rights to reverse decisions taken (via referenda), and initiate laws opposed by the professional politicians (via initiatives), both goals can be achieved at the same time. The same holds for basic human rights which improve the ordinary citizens' position *vis-à-vis* the politicians.

To generally and deeply mistrust the 'classe politique' as done in the works of Hume, Mill, Brennan and Buchanan, and reflected by their constitutional proposals, comes at a price. The Crowding-Out Effect which transforms average citizens with an average level of civic virtue into politicians which are induced to have a low sense of civic duty. A selection effect accentuates the Crowding-Out Effect: persons with particularly low civic virtue are especially attracted to a political career because they are not burdened by mistrusting constitutional rules. The price of having politicians with low civic virtue consists in the cost of the safeguards to prevent the exploitative behaviour against ordinary citizens.

Complete contracts do not provide a solution, as they are impossible particularly in the public sphere. Consequently, trust is even more important in politics and law than elsewhere (see, for example, Cooter, 1994). Even the most extensive systems of controls cannot prevent some extent of exploitative behaviour by politicians; it would moreover be too costly to install. The cost of such distrustful public laws directed against politicians must be compared to a constitution which projects the notion that politicians are persons with at least average civic virtue, if not, indeed a higher level.[2] While this trust will be exploited by some, politicians are not a negative selection among the citizens, and citizens do not lower their morale once they engage in a political career (that is, no Crowding-Out Effect is induced). This has the added advantage that politicians acting as knaves are subject to the social control of other politicians who are likely to be endowed with particularly good information to detect and counteract such behaviour. Even if the damage imposed on the rest of society by politicians as knaves is accepted in the form presented by Brennan and Buchanan (1983), the cost just outlined of a mistrusting constitution suggests that the public laws should (*ceteris paribus*) be less strict than suggested by them.

Not all strict public laws lead, however, to harmful consequences. First of all, regulations which prevent free riding by others, and establish fairness and equity (see Young, 1994) serve to maintain civic virtue. Secondly, the effect of the constitutional provisions on civic virtue depends on the conditions for crowding-out to occur outlined in Chapter 4. Distrustful public laws undermine civic virtues the more strongly

(i)   the closer the politically relevant interactions between the citizens are. In small scale, federalist political units laws distrusting citizens crowd out civic virtues more strongly than in a large, mostly anonymous setting;

(ii) the more participatory the political system has historically been. When distrustful laws are introduced in such a setting, the citizens' civic virtues are more strongly undermined than in a political unit in which the citizens have never experienced such freedom;

(iii) the more extensive the basic attitude implied by the constitution is that 'every citizen is free riding and cheating anyway', and the constitution leaves little or no room to distinguish between normal citizens honouring their duties towards the state and knaves. A constitution which does not invite and induce citizens to cooperate voluntarily with government agencies in order to produce public goods of various kinds[3] tends to crowd out civic virtues;

(iv)   the more the constitutional rules hand out rewards contingent on the 'right' kind of behaviour. This is the case if civic virtue is not taken to be a matter of course but has to be actively revealed by the citizens. Democratic countries which can rely on at least a basic level of civic virtues of their citizens, do not find it necessary to have constitutional rules forcing citizens to show actively and continually that they 'love' their country and constitution. Totalitarian constitutions of both fascist and communist kind, on the other hand, require that the population constantly declares its unconditional support for the political system, and the constitution.

As a result of being constantly forced to pledge allegiance to the political system in order to share in its benefits, there is little room for its voluntary support. Civic virtues are crowded out and the constitution is only observed as far as a strictly material calculation of benefits and cost dictate. When the political system is no longer able to provide the expected benefits, the constitution as a public good is no longer observed and rapidly collapses (for a related, but not identical argument, see Kuran, 1989). This helps to explain the sudden breakdown of such totalitarian ideologies as the Third Reich, fascist Italy, and the communist states in Eastern Europe.

Specific laws and government interventions decrease the civic values of citizens in so far as the Spill-Over Effect applies. Rules that drive out citizens' willingness to contribute to a national task (for instance, in the case of a NIMBY-problem) endanger the acceptance of other national tasks. This has happened in Switzerland where the citizens of a particular commune were induced to accept a nuclear waste disposal site by being offered a substantial monetary contribution (see Chapter 8; Oberholzer-Gee *et al.*, 1995). As a result the citizens of *other* communes are now not prepared to accept *any* NIMBY-project without very high monetary compensation. The question is whether sufficient tax money can be raised to make the Relative Price Effect of the compensation dominate the Crowding-Out Effect. Interestingly enough, Crowding Theory suggests that NIMBY-problems cannot be solved by force because civic virtue is thereby also crowded out and the Spill-Over Effect equally applies.

III EMPIRICALLY TESTING THE THEORY

Attempts to measure the effect of different constitutional conditions on citizens' civic virtue are necessarily faced with great difficulties and uncertainties, and there is only partial evidence available. Most promising are indirect approaches by looking at revealed behaviour. This method has been used to measure tax morale, an important component of civic duty. Econometric tax research has well established that tax paying behaviour cannot be explained in a satisfactory way without taking tax morale into account. Thus, based on the American Internal Revenue Service's Taxpayer Compliance Maintenance Program, Graetz and Wilde (1985, p. 358) conclude that 'the high compliance rate can only be explained either by taxpayers' (...) commitment to the responsibilities of citizenship and respect for the law or lack of opportunity for tax evasion'. The same authors (with Reinganum, 1986) attribute the observed falling tax compliance in the United States to the erosion of tax ethics.[4] As will be shown below, the extent of tax evasion in Switzerland cannot be explained by expected punishment. Indeed, compared to the size of the fine, and the probability of being apprehended, Swiss people would have to cheat much more on taxes than is actually observed. Hence tax morale is an important factor reducing tax evasion in that country, too.

The extent of tax morale depends on the type of constitution existing (see more fully, Pommerehne and Frey, 1993). It is hypothesized, and empirically tested, that the more extensive the citizens' direct political participation possibilities are, the higher is intrinsic motivation in the form of tax morale. Switzerland presents a suitable test case because the various cantons have different degrees of political participation possibilities. It is hypothesized that the more extended political participation possibilities in the form of citizens' meetings, obligatory and optional referenda and initiatives are, the higher is tax morale and (*ceteris paribus*) tax compliance. On the basis of these participation characteristics, about one third of the 26 Swiss cantons are classified as pure direct democracies (*D*), another third as pure representative democracies (*R*), and the rest satisfy only some of the characteristics. A cross section/time series (for the years 1965, 1970, 1978, i.e. 78 observations) multiple regression explaining the part of income not declared Y_{nd} yields the following results[5] (*t*-values in parentheses):

$$Y_{nd} = 7.17 - 3.52\,p - 2.42f + 0.79*t - 0.36*d - 2.72\,Y(ln) + 0.57**NY$$
$$\quad\quad (-1.98)\ (-0.62)\ (2.10)\ (-2.51)\ (-0.30)\quad\quad (2.98)$$

$$-1.09*A - 7.70**D$$
$$(-2.53)\quad (-3.80)$$

R^2(adj.) = 0.69, *d.f.* = 41, *F* = 11.08

*,** indicate statistical significance at the 95% and 99% levels, respectively.

$$Y_{nd} = 8.98 - 3.22\,p - 2.32f + 0.59\,t - 0.42**d + 1.03\,Y(ln) + 0.60**NY$$
$$\quad\quad (-1.72)\ (-0.36)\ (1.70)\ (-3.47)\quad (0.29)\quad\quad (3.07)$$

$$-0.82\,A + 4.02*R$$
$$(-1.93)\quad (2.23)$$

R^2(adj.) = 0.65, *d.f.* = 41, *F* = 9.43

The explanatory variables are:

p = probability of detection (the number of individual income tax audits per 1000 tax payers)
f = penalty tax rate (fine)
t = mean marginal tax rate
d = income deduction possibilities
$Y(ln)$ = per capita income (in natural log.)
NY = non-wage income
A = old-age taxpayers' share
D = pure direct democracies
R = pure representative democracies.

The coefficients of the variables indicating the type of democracy (D, R) – the other variables are used to control for other influences[6] – have the theoretically expected signs and are statistically highly significant. In cantons with a high degree of direct political control by the citizens (*D*), tax morale is (*ceteris paribus*) higher. The part of income concealed falls short of the mean of all cantons by 7.7 percentage points. In absolute terms, the average amount of income concealed is about CHF 1600 (per taxpayer) less than the mean income concealed in all cantons. In contrast, in cantons with a low degree of direct democratic control (*R*), tax morale is (*ceteris paribus*) lower. The part of concealed income is four percentage points higher than the average income gap, and the mean income undeclared exceeds the mean of all cantons by about CHF 1500. The estimation results are consistent with the hypothesis that greater democratic participation possibilities lead to higher civic virtue as reflected in tax payer behaviour (for corresponding evidence for the United States see, for example, Smith, 1992 and Kinsey, 1992).

The empirical evidence collected for Switzerland can be generalized. In a broad sense, two kinds of tax systems can be distinguished: one is based on the premise that the citizens are responsible persons, and that in principle they are prepared to contribute to the provision of public goods and the redistribution of income by the state, provided this process is reasonably efficient and fair (see, for example, Smith, 1992).The corresponding tax laws allow the citizens to declare their own income and to make generalized deductions. The tax statements are in principle accepted as trustworthy, and the tax authority bears the burden of proof if it doubts the declarations.

The second type of tax system starts from the assumption that all citizens want to exploit the tax laws to the fullest, and cheat whenever they can. The corresponding tax laws deduct the taxes directly from gross income, and the citizens are charged to claim back from the government depending on the deductions the tax authorities grant. In the whole process the burden of proof always lies with the individual citizen.

The economic approach to taxation has centred on deterrence, following the influential article by Allingham and Sandmo (1972) based on Becker's theory of crime (1968). Recently, the perspective has changed. Thus Slemrod summarizes his authoritative book on *Why People Pay Taxes* (1992, p. 7) by stating: '... there ... is a change in perspective away from deterring noncompliance toward positive encouragement for compliance – and emphasis on the "carrot" for compliance rather than the "stick" for noncompliance'.

The two basic types of tax systems can be empirically associated with the general level of civic virtue and tax evasion in particular countries (Schmölders, 1960; 1970; Strümpel, 1969). A trusting tax system, a correspondingly high tax morale and relatively low tax evasion exist in the United States and in Switzerland. Econometric research on taxation has indeed revealed for these two countries that the citizens' willingness to pay taxes cannot be explained by an expected utility calculus based on the probability of detection and magnitude of fine.[7] A distrusting tax system obtains in countries such as the Federal Republic of Germany, France and Italy where tax morale is low and tax evasion is relatively large (Frey and Weck-Hanneman, 1984).

Another test of the Crowding-Out Effect of public laws and institutions looks at wages in the government sector. The fact that government employees in many countries are prepared to work for a significantly lower salary (for evidence see, for instance, Poterba and Rueben, 1994) may be attributed to the higher intrinsic motivation of the selection of people seeking employment in the public sector.[8] An example would be those teachers who want to work in government schools because they believe in the virtue of public education for society. The increasing tendency to closely supervise government employees and to curtail their discretionary room has crowded out their work morale which is consistent with a continuous reduction of private sector wage premiums (Poterba and Rueben, 1994). The 'New Public Management' makes an effort to prevent such unfavourable consequences by supporting public officials' intrinsic motivation. One of the means to achieve this result is more discretionary room accorded to them in order to achieve the goals of public activity.

A third way to test the influence of government rules on civic virtues looks at the cost of financing public expenditures in terms of interest rates for government bonds. It has been argued (Schultz and Weingast, 1994) that democracies find it less costly to finance themselves than authoritarian political systems because nations under a democratic constitution are more credible, and therefore more likely to pay back their debts. The observation of lower cost of finance under a democratic constitution is, however, also fully consistent with Crowding Theory: the citizens have a higher level of trust in, and attachment to, their state and are therefore more willing to grant credit to their state at more favourable financial conditions than are the subjects who feel oppressed by their constitution.

On a more general level, there is a cumulative body of research indicating that people's perceptions of how they are treated by the authorities strongly affect their evaluation of authorities and laws, and their willingness to cooperate with them (for example, Bardach and Kagan, 1982; Lind and Tyler, 1988; Tyler and McGraw, 1986). Citizens who consider the constitution and its laws, and the authorities acting on their basis to be fair and to treat them respectfully, tend to be more compliant than those with more negative perceptions of government (for example, Thibaut and Walker, 1976; and for extensive empirical evidence, see Tyler, 1990). Kelman (1992) shows that the extensive use of adversarial institutions for resolving public conflicts (which are prevalent in the United States, for instance, in the court system) tends negatively to affect civic virtue. The incentives of politicians, public officials and citizens to cooperate is therewith made more difficult.

IV CONCLUSION

Preventing knaves from exploiting the political system has not only advantages, but also costs by crowding out civic virtue on which an effective constitution and other public laws crucially depend. Constitutional economics, in contrast, has concentrated on the perennial propensity of individuals to behave as opportunists and to free-ride. A viable constitution must indeed guard against such behaviour, not least because it undermines civic virtue if it becomes widespread. This chapter emphasizes, however, a different aspect: care must be taken not to design a system of laws fundamentally distrusting citizens and politicians. If the government rules provoke the perception that everyone is a knave irrespective of his or her behaviour, civic virtues tend to be driven out. Public laws designed for the worst possible behaviour and not average behaviour run the risk of destroying the crucially important positive attitude of the citizens and politicians towards their constitution which is efficient to maintain, and vital for, its long-run survival.

NOTES

1. It should be made clear that Brennan and Buchanan are well aware of, and even stress, the role of moral principles; they explicitly and repeatedly refer in their 1983

article to moral considerations as constraining individuals' behaviour in the political context. Buchanan (1985, p. 1) states, for instance, that: 'A positive, empirical theory of the operation of moral rules is in order even if we want to leave the preaching to the moralists'. More recently, he even argues that 'If the necessary personal constraints are not present ... increased resource investment in both policing and preaching becomes more productive' (Buchanan, 1994, p. 25). The essential point in our context is, however, that Buchanan and Brennan do not take into account any causal effect of the (type of) constitution on citizens' morale.

2. Both views may be observed in reality: in classical Greece and Rome the reigning notion was that politicians are men of particularly high virtue. In contrast, the general notion of a politician's character held by average Americans today is bleak: they are indeed taken to be knaves, or crooks.

3. This has been termed 'coproduction', see, for example, Whitaker (1980), Neiman (1989). It has been empirically shown to be of great importance for instance in the case of obeying safety belt laws (Curtis *et al.*, 1991).

4. Further evidence can be found, among others, in Schwartz and Orleans (1967), Lewis (1982), Roth, Scholz and Witte (1989), Pyle (1990), and Slemrod (1992).

5. Due to multicollinearity between D and R ($r = 0.6$) two separate equations including D and R have been estimated.

6. It may be observed that while many coefficients are statistically significant and have the theoretically expected signs, the probability of detection p and the size of the fine f are not statistically significant at the conventional levels, that is, it cannot be presumed that deterrence works.

7. The implied risk aversion to account for observed behaviour would be incredibly higher than anywhere else empirically observed, see Skinner and Slemrod (1985) and Alm *et al.* (1995) for the United States, and Pommerehne and Frey (1993) for Switzerland. Econometric tax research has at least so far not been able to identify a consistent, and quantitatively significant negative influence of deterrence on tax evasion (see, e.g. Roth, Scholz and Witte, 1989; Cowell, 1990; Slemrod 1992).

8. Alternative explanations for the unobserved factor producing the wage differential such as higher fringe benefits or lower work intensity are, of course, possible.

SUGGESTED FURTHER READINGS

The consequences of treating citizens as knaves, or crooks, for the design of institutions has been analysed by

Brennan, Geoffrey and James M. Buchanan (1985), *The Reason of Rules. Constitutional Political Economy*, Cambridge, Mass.: Cambridge University Press.

The role of trust and civic virtue is emphasized by

Tyler, Tom R. (1990), *Why People Obey the Law*, New Haven and London: Yale University Press.

Mansbridge, Jane (1994), 'Public Spirit in Political Systems', in Henry J. Aaron, Thomas E. Mann and Timothy Taylor (eds), *Values and Public Policy*, Washington: Brookings, 146–72.

The extent of satisfaction of the citizens with the state and the democratic institutions are empirically analysed in

Klingenmann, Hans-Dieter and Dieter Fuchs (eds) (1995), *Citizens and the State*, Oxford: Oxford University Press.

An extensive survey of tax paying behaviour and the role of tax morale is
  given in
Slemrod, Joel (ed.) (1992), *Why People Pay Taxes. Tax Compliance and Enforcement*, Ann Arbor: University of Michigan Press.

7. Environmental policy

I THE ISSUE

Until the 1970s it was generally taken to be a matter of course that the government sets laws and regulations to reduce pollution and to protect the environment. In contrast, the more recent theory of environmental economics strongly suggests that the use of incentive instruments, which exploit the Price Effect, constitutes the most efficient and desirable policy. A recent survey on environmental policy (Hahn, 1989, p. 95) notes that 'the two tools which have received widespread support from the economics community (are) marketable permits and emission charges'. Environmental incentive instruments count among the most successful applications of economic theory (Faulhaber and Baumol, 1988; Cropper and Oates, 1992). During the last few years, emission charges and tradeable effluent licences moved from being an academic proposal to being part of the policy programme of many parties across the whole political spectrum. Nevertheless, incentive instruments are little used all over the world (Hahn, 1989), and an OECD study (1994) also sees little prospect that they will be used on an extensive scale in the future.

The economic arguments brought forward in favour of incentive-based environmental instruments are accepted in this chapter. Using the Relative Price Effect in order to improve our natural environment makes a lot of sense. It is argued, however, that the favourable outcomes attributed to environmental incentive instruments *depend on particular conditions*. The domain of favourable outcomes is restricted because the introduction of incentive instruments under identifiable conditions leads to a countervailing effect. In these cases, the application of emission charges or tradeable licences leads to a perverse effect, and environmental conditions worsen.

The argument does not rest on the (well-known) transaction costs which may arise, that is, that the costs of administering and monitoring incentive instruments may be so high that they outweigh the benefits achieved by their application. Rather, the argument is based on the Crowding-Out Effect stating that there exist conditions under which incentive instruments undermine environmental morale, tending to lead to a less environmentally conscious behaviour.

The pertinent question analysed in this chapter is: which of the two effects – the Price Effect or the Crowding-Out Effect – prevails? It is identified under what conditions the Crowding-Out Effect becomes relevant and may dominate the Price Effect. The analysis has important consequences for environmental policy.

II ENVIRONMENTAL MORALE AS INTRINSIC MOTIVATION

There exists an extensive literature on environmental ethics.[1] It is, however, almost exclusively normatively oriented, and there are only few serious explanatory studies about the extent of environmental morale in the population.[2]

A positive approach to environmental ethics starts from the net cost (that is, the cost after deducting possible benefits) of pursuing ethical concerns in individual behaviour. Following North (1990, pp. 43–4), who suggested a downward sloping demand curve for ideology in general, the extent of environmental morale applied is taken to be the larger the lower the personal net cost of doing so (Figure 7.1). It is thus suggested that individuals are prepared to apply much environmental morale in their behaviour when it costs them little (see Kliemt, 1986 and Kirchgässner, 1992 on 'low cost decisions'). The more costly it gets, the lower the weight of moral concerns. When the cost is very high, only ecological extremists still follow the principles of environmental ethics while ordinary people find a lot of reasons why they should desist from doing so.

It is crucial to identify carefully what 'cost' means in this context. A firm under perfectly competitive conditions has high cost (it faces bankruptcy) if it follows environmental norms and other firms do not. This statement must, however, be qualified in various respects. First of all, to act in an environmentally conscious way may pay for a firm if it can thereby increase its sales or circumvent a boycott or other trouble from environmental action groups and other stakeholders. Such behaviour may also be warranted if it pre-empts impending government environmental policy and helps to be on good terms with the govern-

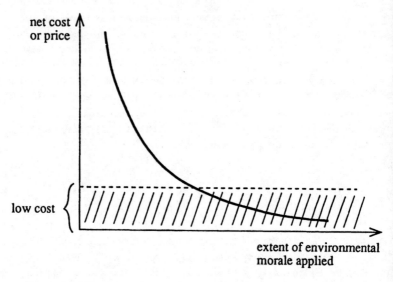

Figure 7.1   The demand curve for environmental morale

ment and its administration on which the firm depends, for example, on future orders. Finally, few firms are subject to perfectly competitive conditions; rather, most of them have sufficient discretionary room to deviate to some extent from profit maximizing behaviour, and to follow ecological norms.

The survival argument just discussed for firms is relevant for individuals in wartime or in poor developing countries where people die from hunger if they do not fully exploit all opportunities. Under these conditions, the cost of environmental morale is exceedingly high. It cannot therefore be expected that such persons refuse, for example, to burn wood or plunder the tree stock even if they are aware that there is an unfortunate outcome in the long run and the soil is eroded.

For most people in industrial countries, however, the crude survival argument is not relevant. For (professional) environmental activists, such as employees of Greenpeace, the pursuit of environmental ethics is even connected with positive net benefits in terms of prestige, attention, income, and promotion prospects. The same holds for persons living in groups and contexts in which ecological concerns are taken as a kind of religion. Even for individuals not living under such conditions, environmental morale may be connected with low or even zero cost in so far as small actions are concerned. Examples are collecting household refuse according to ecological principles (for example, separating glass or batteries), or abstaining from throwing trash on the road. Indeed, Baumol and Oates (1979, pp. 296–9) find that when there is an extraordinary shortage of water, people are prepared to reduce their consumption in the short run. In that case, moral suasion and appeals work to some extent. For post-catastrophic behaviour, De Alessi (1983) has empirically shown that people are prepared to help each other on purely moral motives. But this motivation vanishes rather quickly, especially when help comes in from outside. In another important case the cost of pursuing environmental morale is low, namely voting in elections and popular referenda. Each voter only has a minuscule impact on the total vote outcome and therefore casting a vote in favour of environmental projects is nearly costless.

There are thus important circumstances in which individuals and firms pursue environmental morale. This behaviour is a particular manifestation of intrinsic motivation. Crowding-Out Effects therefore become potentially relevant for environmental policy.

III WHEN ARE INCENTIVE INSTRUMENTS EFFECTIVE?

How well environmental incentive instruments work depends in our context on two factors: (i) the importance of environmental morale for behaviour, which is determined by the associated cost; and (ii) the intensity to which the incentive instruments are used, that is, the extent of external intervention affecting individuals. The interaction of these two determinants is analysed by distinguishing in each case, for simplicity, only a low level and a high level. Table 7.1 illustrates the outcome expected when the cost of environmental morale and external intervention are either low or high. The four paradigmatic outcomes are now discussed in sequence.

1 Low cost of environmental morale, low extent of intervention
Under these conditions, individuals and firms exhibit a high amount of environmental morale. As the corresponding behaviour is not influenced by the application of emission charges or tradeable licences, the environment will be preserved. The area in which these conditions hold may be called 'voluntaristic environmentalism'. Examples are the separation of household refuse or careful disposal of wastepaper or chewing

Table 7.1   Environmental outcomes

		cost of applying environmental morale	
		low	high
extent of external intervention	low	(1) environment preserved	(2) environment destroyed
(application of incentive instruments)	high	(3) countervailing effects on environment	(4) environment preserved

gums in public places. Voluntaristic environmental activities have been rather neglected by economists but play a considerable role in everyday behaviour. However, non-economists often tend to overestimate its importance. Many environmentalists seem to believe that most environmental issues belong to that area.

2   High cost of environmental morale, low extent of intervention
In this area, environmental morale is not active because it burdens individuals and firms too heavily. Behaviour is not influenced by the application of environmental instruments. There is no internal nor external motivation to protect the environment, and it therefore tends to be destroyed. Examples for this constellation are:

- Environmental behaviour in planned economies where the cost of behaving morally is high as production plans have to be met or even surpassed (at least in formal terms). At the same time, central economic policy does not care for ecological issues. As a result, grave environmental damages occur. After the breakdown of the communist systems, we are now fully aware of this outcome.
- The destruction of woods and the consequent soil erosion in developing countries where individuals cannot afford to behave

morally towards the environment, and where there is little or no environmental intervention by the government.

- Newly arising market economies without environmental policies where people enter the consumption phase and subjectively find it costly to behave according to environmental norms (in particular because of the need to keep up with the 'Joneses').

- International environmental problems such as the greenhouse effect or the preservation of oceans where many people find it difficult to establish a strong connection between their own behaviour and the global ecological outcomes, and where environmental morale is therefore costly. At the same time, the public good nature of the problems makes it hard, or even impossible, for governments to cooperate and to intervene externally.

3 Low cost of environmental morale, high extent of intervention

When incentive instruments are used to fight environmental pollution, and individuals initially follow environmental morale, a Crowding-Out Effect is induced. The question is, whether the destructive effect on intrinsic environmental motivation is stronger than the behavioural change induced by the Price Effect of the environmental policy instruments. The outcome depends on the six conditions generally identified in Chapter 4 as prerequisites for the Crowding-Out Effect:

(a) In *personalized relationships* the Crowding-Out Effect is strong. This condition may apply for ecological activity groups which strongly rely on the cohesion between particular persons, and where the government intervenes to steer environmental behaviour via relative price changes. Such external intervention is likely to destroy such groups' cohesion because their *raison d'être* is fundamentally questioned. If the government fulfils the tasks previously undertaken by such groups, their members may well lose their sense of purpose and direct their intrinsic motivation to other issues. Whether the environment improves or degrades is open.

(b) For *interesting tasks* the Crowding-Out Effect is strong. People who follow the standards of environmental ethics in their behaviour because they find the underlying ecological issues fascinating, experience a severe loss of motivation when the same task is performed by an externally imposed policy instrument.

(c) When environmental problems have been cared for by *self-organization*, an external intervention destroys any intrinsic motivation the participants have. As Ostrom (1990) has shown, many common property resource problems have been successfully addressed by self-organization, but her research also reveals that an outside intervention by government often has disastrous consequences on morale.

(d)   When incentive instruments fail to *differentiate* between persons with high and low environmental ethics, the Crowding-Out Effect is strong. Examples are firms which use their discretionary room voluntarily to safeguard the environment but which are nevertheless subjected to the same regime as firms which do not care for ecological issues. This exists when an environmental tax for administrative reasons is based on the sector's average emission. In this case environmental conscious behaviour is not recognized, and it is likely that the managers of those firms react by adjusting their pollution to the sector's average level (see Wicke 1991, pp. 369–70).

(e)   The more strongly *rewards are contingent on behaviour*, the more environmental morale is driven out. Economic incentive instruments are based on a close relationship with behaviour so that the Price Effect works at its best. At the same time, however, this makes intrinsic motivation unnecessary, crowding it out. An example is the pricing of household refuse according to quantity. While each household has an extrinsic incentive to minimize its quantity, environmental morale becomes superfluous.

(f)   Environmental morale is crowded out when the environmental policy instruments applied *fail to acknowledge* the affected persons' intrinsic motivation to protect the environment. This Crowding-Out Effect particularly applies in the case of tradeable licences. Licences allow a specific amount of pollution and do not morally condemn damaging the environment as long as the emitter stays within these limits. In this particular sense, once a licence has been acquired, there is a 'licence to pollute'. All intrinsically motivated environmental concerns by this procedure are implicitly declared irrelevant. An environmental policy built on tradeable licences thus actively undermines environmental ethics (a similar argument has been proffered by Kelman, 1981).

4   High cost of environmental morale, high extent of intervention

When these conditions apply, environmental incentive instruments work well. Environmental morale does not affect behaviour, so that the Price

Effect of emission charges and tradeable licences fully determines behaviour, provided the other conditions necessary for the application of these instruments apply. In particular: (i) the transaction cost of applying incentive instruments must be so low that it pays to employ them; (ii) politicians and administrators must understand the working of incentive instruments to apply them properly; (iii) interest groups losing from an efficient environmental policy must not have the power to block or undermine incentive instruments; and (iv) the public officials must be made to effectively apply the incentive instruments which is not trivial because bureaucrats often prefer direct regulations giving them more discretionary power.

IV CONSEQUENCES FOR ENVIRONMENTAL POLICY

Our analysis helps us to understand why the environmental incentive instruments have been applied so little for such a long time, why even today their use is quite restricted and why experts do not expect that they will play a major role in future environmental policy. There are certainly many politico-economic reasons why such instruments are little applied (see Frey, 1992b; Weck-Hannemann, 1994), but our discussion suggests an additional reason: people are aware of the damaging effects incentive instruments may have on environmental morale. They abhor the moral vacuum produced by incentive instruments.

People may also be concerned about the Spill-Over Effect prompted by the destruction of environmental morale induced by incentive instruments. The environment is seen as a whole which is supported by the fact that in many countries there are green parties and interest groups based on this one issue (Parkin, 1989). Decision-makers fear that the use of incentive instruments has a double effect: the quality of the environment is improved in those areas in which environmental charges and/or tradeable licences are applicable, but environmental quality is lowered in all other areas because environmental morale is weakened or completely destroyed. The destruction of environmental morale hampers individuals' willingness to accept any kind of action to fight pollution, that is, political support for environmental policies would also be negatively affected. This explains why even those groups who claim to fight for green interests may oppose pricing as an instrument of environmental policy: it would erode the basis of their popular support.

Provided the Crowding-Out and Spill-Over Effects are sizeable, the consequences of using incentive instruments are counterproductive and overall environmental quality falls. Under these conditions, their application leads to the opposite of what was intended.

Pollution is mainly looked at as a moral issue by many decision-makers as well as the general population (see, for example, Blinder, 1987, pp. 147–54). In the United States where the use of pricing for resource allocation is more accepted than it is in Europe or Japan,[3] motivation crowding-out and spill-over are of less importance, leading to the proposition that incentive instruments in environmental policy are used more in the United States than in Europe. Another proposition derived from the analysis is that the Crowding-Out and Spill-Over Effects apply more strongly for consumers than for managers of firms who cannot pursue environmental morale if they are in a strongly competitive situation. It is, moreover, to be expected that firms supplying intermediate products are less subject to motivational effects of incentive instruments.

Finally, the theoretical analysis suggests that instruments are preferred which entail a moral condemnation of pollution. This holds for regulations and, even more so, subsidies which reward environmentally conscious behaviour. In contrast, tradeable permits and charges imply that no moral wrong is connected with pollution. This leads to the empirical propositions that environmental incentive instruments are little used for a policy directed at consumers but rather at firms, and in particular, at firms supplying intermediate products and being in an oligopolistic or monopolistic position. These propositions are consistent with the evidence (OECD 1989; Hahn, 1989): environmental charges or tradeable permits are rarely if ever applied directly to consumers, but rather to firms. Indeed, the only successful application of tradeable permits in the United States is to oligopolistic petroleum refineries to induce them to reduce the lead content of gasoline (Hahn, 1989). On the other hand, regulations, subsidies, and deposit-refunds which tend to support environmental morale are predominantly used in all countries. On the other hand, those pricing instruments which tend to be interpreted by actors as a direct or indirect 'licence to pollute' are little used in all countries.

What can be concluded about the desirable environmental policy? There are definite limits to the application of pricing to fight pollution. Relative price changes strongly influence behaviour but there are areas in which incentive instruments are much less effective owing to the countervailing effect of crowding out environmental morale. Those areas of environmental policy have been identified where the Crowding-Out Effect is likely to be strong, and where it can safely be neglected.

Environmental incentive instruments should be modified in order to minimize possible Crowding-Out Effects. Most importantly, economists should change the attitude with which they argue for incentive instruments. Most people concerned about the environment find it cynical to state that once one has paid a price, one is free to damage the environment. This type of thinking and arguing (while perfectly acceptable among professional economists) is strongly objected by most non-economists. Indeed, Blinder (1987, p. 148) has found that 'environmentalists ... want business to reduce pollution because it is the right thing to do, not because it is in their financial interest'. Economists should acknowledge that the motivational structure of individuals is more complex than in their traditional model. Once they accept that behaviour is not solely motivated by extrinsic inducements, but to a significant extent also depends on intrinsic motivation, they must become aware that their cynicism has considerable cost by damaging environmental morale. Incentive instruments should be applied in conjunction with statements stressing that a person's or firm's intrinsic motivation to protect the natural environment is highly valued, and the use of the incentive instruments should mainly be suggested for areas where environmental ethics is weak or non-existent. What is proposed is a partial rehabilitation of moral appeals in environmental policy – without giving up incentive instruments.

NOTES

1. For example, Attfield (1993), Miller (1990), Des Jardins (1993). There is also a specialized professional journal of *Environmental Ethics*.
2. A major shortcoming of the few studies devoted to a positive analysis is that they do not clearly distinguish environmentally conscious behaviour induced by benefit–cost considerations, and that induced by 'pure' ethical considerations; see, for example, Rodman (1983) and Des Jardins (1993).
3. One piece of evidence supporting this statement is that American economists, other factors held constant, have a stronger preference for pricing solutions than European economists (Pommerehne, *et al.* 1984). American workers are more prepared to accept the price system than their Japanese and European counterparts, see also Beer *et al.* (1984, p. 116) and Aoki (1990).

SUGGESTED FURTHER READINGS

A good introduction into the principles of environmental economics is
Baumol, William J. and Wallace E. Oates (1979), *Economics, Environmental
  Policy, and the Quality of Life*, Englewood Cliffs, N.J.: Prentice Hall.
More recent overviews are provided in
Cropper, Maureen L. and Wallace E. Oates (1992), 'Environmental Econom-
  ics: A Survey', *Journal of Economic Literature*, **30**, 675–740.
OECD (1994), *Integrating Environment and Economics: The Role of Eco-
  nomic Instruments*, Paris: Organization for Economic Cooperation and De-
  velopment.
Empirical evidence on environmental policy is provided in
Hahn, Robert W. (1989), 'Economic Prescriptions for Environmental Prob-
  lems. How the Patients Followed the Doctor's Orders', *Journal of Economic
  Perspectives*, **3** (Spring), 95–114.
Normative aspects towards nature are discussed by
Des Jardins, Joseph R. (1993), *Environmental Ethics*, Belmont: Wadsworth.
The possibility that economic incentive instruments may damage environmen-
tal morale has been discussed by
Kelman, Steven (1981), *What Price Incentives? Economists and the Environ-
  ment*, Boston: Auburn House.

8. Siting policy, or: the NIMBY-problem

with Felix Oberholzer-Gee

This chapter presents an additional econometric test for the motivation Crowding-Out Effect in the context of an important real life issue: the siting of locally unwanted facilities (the so-called 'Not In My Backyard' or NIMBY-problem). Where the Crowding-Out Effect persists, a monetary compensation for accepting the undesired project is not simply additive to any altruistic motivation to permit construction. Instead, such intrinsic motivation is partially or totally destroyed if price incentives are introduced. If motivation crowding-out is taken into account, a higher level of monetary compensation is needed to achieve any given result. In view of the high (dead weight) cost of financing such incentives (see Browning, 1987), it may become inefficient to introduce price incentives at all. There are even conditions under which the willingness to accept a site is reduced by offering a payment.

I THE SITING PROBLEM

The individual's willingness to accept locally unwanted facilities depends both on extrinsic and intrinsic factors of motivation. For many different projects and major capital investments, a wide consensus exists that they are worth being undertaken. But no community is prepared to tolerate their vicinity. Such 'nimbyistic' behaviour is well documented in cases where communities object to the siting of hazardous waste disposal facilities, the construction of freeways, airports, prisons, and clinics for the physically or mentally handicapped (for example, Easterling and Kunreuther, 1995; Portney, 1991). In these instances, citizens generally support a collective enterprise, but they are not prepared to have it carried out in their own neighbourhood. This is not surprising as the host community has to carry most of the cost of such projects in terms of risk of future damage (explosions, nuclear emissions, chemical leaks, and so on) and current costs such as noise, environmental degradation, and reductions in amenities.

Economists have a handy tool to solve the NIMBY-problem. As the aggregate net benefits of undertaking the project are positive, one must simply redistribute them in an appropriate way. The communities that are prepared to accept the undesired project within their borders must be compensated in such a way as to make their net benefits positive, while the other communities must be taxed to raise the sum of compensation.[1] However, this policy recommendation underestimates the true costs of introducing price incentives in that it fails to take into account the detrimental effects of motivation crowding-out.

A citizen living in a prospective host community will incur certain costs, such as health risks, negative economic impacts or lower property values, if the project is built in his or her community. Monetary compensation raises the level of support by lowering the marginal cost of accepting the project. Detrimental economic effects of noxious facilities can thus be offset by financial compensation. This is the standard Price Effect. In contrast, when monetary rewards undermine intrinsic motivation, the marginal benefit of supporting the siting is lowered. If this motivation Crowding-Out Effect dominates the standard Price Effect, the external monetary intervention reduces a citizen's optimal level of support. Using price incentives becomes more costly because increased support due to higher monetary incentives must be traded off against losing support as notions of civic duty are crowded out. If the Crowding-Out dominates the Price Effect of financial rewards, compensation strengthens the local opposition.

Based on the conditions identified in Chapter 4, which determine the size of the motivation Crowding Effect, the following hypotheses can be advanced:

(1) The higher a citizen's initial sense of civic duty, the more strongly intrinsic motivation is crowded out when compensation is introduced. Whether local residents perceive a facility to be in the national or regional interest at all is largely an empirical question we will have to answer in the next section. However, if this is the case, we hypothesize that introducing monetary compensation will not automatically lead to higher levels of support for the noxious facility.

(2) If citizens are to remain intrinsically motivated to serve their country and accept thankless tasks, they must be convinced that

the burdens are generally shared in a fair manner. If a community feels it is being used as a dumping ground for all sorts of noxious facilities, we can hardly expect it to exhibit much intrinsic motivation in contributing to the solution of siting problems. On the other hand, if the site selection process is perceived to be fair, we expect to find more intrinsically motivated citizens. The better the acceptability of the site selection process, the larger the motivation crowding effect will be, *ceteris paribus*.

(3) In order to preserve one's intrinsic motivation, it is essential to believe that the action undertaken corresponds to personal convictions. We expect citizens who emphasize the importance of technically and socially sound solutions to react negatively to the introduction of price incentives if they feel that money is used to cover up technical or social weaknesses of the facility. Since many facilities cannot be proven to be reasonably safe, the introduction of price incentives tends to crowd out the intrinsic motivation of this group of people.

II ECONOMETRIC TEST

The three hypotheses are tested by analysing the reaction to monetary compensation offered for the acceptance of a nuclear waste repository. We conducted a survey among the general population in Switzerland in Spring 1993. In a one-hour personal interview, 511 persons were asked about their attitudes regarding the siting of nuclear waste repositories in Switzerland. Our survey does not, and cannot, analyse actual behaviour. A good number of social scientists, in particular economists, object to the use of verbal statements elicited in surveys, arguing that they are not relevant for behaviour (Diamond and Hausmann, 1994; for a more favourable review of the contingent valuation method, see Mitchell and Carson, 1989). In our case, this point does not seem valid for two reasons. First, verbal statements are a form of behaviour. They are crucial in many areas, especially in bargaining situations and in the political realm. The case we are studying is located in the sphere of democratic politics (in Switzerland siting decisions are taken by referendum and/or town hall meetings). Therefore, the procedure of finding a site contains major bargaining elements that can be captured using the contingent valuation method. Secondly, political protest, also an important part of verbal behaviour, has been shown to be a key determinant in siting decisions for noxious facilities (Hamilton, 1993). Clearly, this situation is much different from the (pure) price system where attitudes and behaviour are less connected, if at all.

We asked all respondents if they were willing to permit the construction of a nuclear waste repository for short-lived, low- and mid-level radioactive waste on the grounds of their community. At the time of the survey, four communities had been singled out as potential locations for such a facility, which will be constructed during the next decade. Three hundred and five respondents lived in one of these communities. The National Cooperative for the Storage of Nuclear Waste, the agency responsible for the siting of the repository, was about to announce its final choice. Thus, the question posed was not far-fetched at all. Not knowing when the results of the survey would be published, respondents not only had a chance to express their opinions, but could possibly influence the siting decision. All empirical results reported here pertain to the 305 respondents who are directly affected by the siting decision.[2]

More than half of the respondents (50.8 per cent) agreed to have the nuclear waste repository built in their community, 44.9 per cent opposed the siting, and 4.3 per cent did not care where the facility was built. Thus, this unfavourable siting decision is widely accepted in spite of the fact that a nuclear waste repository is mostly seen as a heavy burden for the residents of the host community. Nearly 40 per cent of all respondents believed the risk of serious accidents in the facility and ground water contamination to be considerable. Thirty four per cent were convinced that some local residents would die as a result of any environmental contamination, and close to 80 per cent believed that many local residents would suffer long-term effects should any accident occur. More than half of the respondents further expected the developer to withhold vital information and downplay the risk should the environment become contaminated.

In accordance with our model of behaviour, we predict risk estimates and expectations of economic impacts to be major influences on the willingness to accept the siting of a noxious facility. Data for both variables were collected in the survey. In addition, we believe that political considerations are important. The inability to successfully complete the construction of nuclear waste repositories would limit the future prospects of nuclear energy in Switzerland. We therefore expect opponents of nuclear energy to also oppose the construction of waste repositories. The degree of opposition to nuclear energy was measured by asking respondents how they would vote on the 'exit' proposition at the time the survey was conducted. This proposition which demanded the abandonment of all nuclear energy production was put to a national referendum in 1990.

Our model further contains a number of personal characteristics such as political orientation, income, age, and sex. Economic theory, however, does not predict how these variables will influence the willingness to host a noxious facility. In order to empirically test our second proposition, namely, that perceived fairness of the site selection process contributes positively to a sense of civic duty and thus to the willingness to accept the repository, we included a variable which measures the individually perceived acceptability of the current Swiss siting procedure. The respondents who score high on this measure generally think of the Swiss siting procedure as a fair process. As hypothesized above, using acceptable siting methods should win the support of intrinsically motivated citizens. We thus expect a positive sign for this last variable.

Table 8.1 reports the results of a binary logit analysis which seeks to explain why individuals accept a nuclear waste facility. The dependent responses are 'accept' answers. Those who did not care about the construction of a nuclear waste repository were omitted from the analysis.

The predictive power of our model is quite satisfactory. Eighty per cent of all answers are predicted correctly. This approximately represents a 30 per cent gain in correctly predicted answers compared to a completely random model which assigns each observation the same probability of acceptance. A likelihood ratio test of the null hypothesis that all coefficients except the constant are zero rejects this hypothesis.[3]

The results of the binary logit analysis correspond to our theoretical expectations. Higher perceived risk, negative economic impacts, and ownership of a home all decrease the willingness to host a nuclear waste repository. *Ceteris paribus* (holding all other covariates at mean value), the probability of accepting a nuclear waste facility in one's home town decreases by 7.1 per cent with every additional point on the risk scale ('1 = risk very low' to '6 = risk very high'). Respondents who expect negative economic consequences from the construction of a waste facility exhibit a 13 per cent lower probability of acceptance. The negative effect of home ownership on the willingness to accept noxious facilities is explained by the fact that there are no legal provisions that protect homeowners from losses in property value due to the construction of waste repositories. Personal characteristics such as political

Table 8.1   Determinants of acceptance to host a nuclear waste repository when no compensation is paid – results of a binary logit analysis

Independent variables	Willingness to accept facility without compensation	
	Estimate (S.E.)	Change in probability of acceptance (*t*-ratio)
Constant	16.35 (28.03)	
Individual risk estimate	−0.72	−7.1%**
('1 = very low' to '6 = very high'; effect of 1 point increase reported)	(0.13)	(−5.57)
Negative economic impacts expected	−1.32	−13.0%**
(1 = yes, 0 = otherwise)	(0.45)	(−2.95)
Home ownership	−1.25	−12.4%**
(1 = yes, 0 = otherwise)	(0.44)	(−2.83)
'Exit' proposition rejected	1.13	+11.2%**
(1 = yes, 0 = otherwise)	(0.41)	(2.76)
Political orientation	0.05	+1%
('1 = left' to '6 = right')	(0.14)	(0.33)
Income	−0.01	0%
CHF 1000 per month	(0.04)	(−0.33)
Age	−0.01	0%
	(0.01)	(−0.48)
Sex (effect of being female)	−0.33	−3.2%
	(0.39)	(−0.84)
Acceptance of current siting procedure	0.62	+6.2%**
(1 = 'not acceptable at all' to 6 = 'completely acceptable'; effect of 1 point increase reported)	(0.13)	(4.95)

Note:
** = significant at the 99% level
The estimated coefficients can be interpreted as the log of odds-ratios for a dichotomous independent variable. Since these coefficients are not a intuitively meaningful quantity, we provide derivatives indicating changes in the probability of accepting a nuclear waste repository. Holding all independent variables at their mean value, these derivatives show the effect of point for point changes in a single independent variable on the probability of accepting a nuclear waste repository. Thus, the derivative for the risk variable with a value of −7.1% can be interpreted as follows: if two respondents A and B differ only in their risk estimates, A estimating the risk to be 4 points (on a scale from 1 to 6) and B judging it to be 5 points, the probability of accepting a nuclear waste repository is on average 7.1% lower for B than for A. If it were the only difference between A and B that the former owned its home while the latter did not, A's probability of accepting a nuclear waste repository would be 12.4% lower than B's (derivative of −12.4%).[4]

orientation, income, age, education, and sex do not exercise any significant influence.

As hypothesized, the acceptability of the current siting procedure positively contributes to the willingness to permit the construction of noxious facilities. The level of acceptance for the current procedure is rather high (50.8 per cent of all respondents believe the procedure to be acceptable[5]) resulting in an increased willingness to accept the burden in the national interest. So far, we find the standard economic model of behaviour confirmed. The benefits of the nuclear facility – in addition to the satisfaction derived from fulfilling one's civic duty – also consist of economic advantages since the operation of the facility would create 25 local jobs in a relatively small community. In contrast, rising marginal costs reduce the level of support, that is, the willingness to accept the facility.

We now turn to the analysis of changes in the level of external compensation. To this end, we repeated the same question asking our respondents whether they were willing to accept the construction of a nuclear waste repository. This time, however, we added that the Swiss parliament had decided to compensate all residents of the host community. The amount offered varied from CHF 2500 per individual and year (N = 117), to CHF 5000 (N = 102), and CHF 7500 (N = 86).[6] While 50.8 per cent of the respondents agreed to accept the nuclear waste repository without compensation, the level of acceptance drops to 24.6 per cent when compensation is offered. About one quarter of the respondents seem to reject the facility simply because financial compensation is attached to it. The amount of compensation has no significant effect on the level of acceptance.[7] There is further evidence which suggests that it is not the level of compensation which caused so many individuals to decline the offer. Everyone who rejected the first compensation was given a better offer, thereby raising the amount of compensation from CHF 2500 to 3750, from 5000 to 7500, and from 7500 to 10,000. Despite this marked increase, only a single respondent who declined the first compensation was now prepared to accept the higher offer.

Table 8.2 seeks to determine the influence of the previously discussed covariates on the decision to accept a noxious facility when compensation is offered.

While the core economic variables retain a similar influence and the personal characteristics remain statistically insignificant, there are marked changes in two variables. First, the acceptance of the current

Table 8.2   Determinants of acceptance to host a nuclear waste repository when compensation is paid – results of a binary logit analysis

Independent variable	Willingness to accept facility without compensation	
	Estimate (S.E.)	Change in probability of acceptance (*t*-ratio)
Constant	16.78 (22.85)	
Individual risk estimate ('1 = very low' to '6 = very high'; effect of 1 point increase reported)	−0.28 (0.11)	−4.4%** (−2.54)
Negative economic impacts expected (1 = yes, 0 = otherwise)	−1.10 (0.47)	−17.5%* (−2.35)
Home ownership (1 = yes, 0 = otherwise)	−0.59 (0.32)	−9.4% (−1.79)
'Exit' proposition rejected (1 = yes, 0 = otherwise)	−0.21 (0.32)	−3.3% (−0.64)
Political orientation ('1 = left' to '6 = right')	0.13 (0.12)	+2% (1.05)
Income CHF 1000 per month	0.01 (0.03)	0% (0.12)
Age	−0.01 (0.01)	0% (−0.66)
Sex (effect of being female)	−0.23 (0.32)	−3.6% (−0.72)
Acceptance of current siting procedure (1 = 'not acceptable at all' to 6 = 'completely acceptable'; effect of 1 point increase reported)	0.04 (0.10)	+1% (0.42)

Note:
* = significant at the 95% level, ** = significant at the 99% level
The explanatory power of this model is somewhat weaker. Only 68% of all answers are predicted correctly. Again, a likelihood ratio test of the null hypothesis that all coefficients except the constant are zero rejects this hypothesis.[8]

procedure (which does not include compensation) is no longer corre-lated with the willingness to accept the facility when compensation is offered. Compensation, we conclude, fundamentally alters the perceived nature of a siting procedure, and it is not possible to increase levels of acceptance by simply adding 'financial benefit packages', as develop-ers like to call them, to a well-accepted siting scheme. What we ob-serve in this analysis of verbal behaviour represents precisely the type of mechanism postulated by motivation Crowding Theory. While exter-nal intervention, that is, offering compensation, manages to address concerns regarding the costs of a noxious facility, it reduces the intrin-sic motivation to permit the construction of such a facility. In our case, this latter effect even outweighs the benefits of external intervention, thereby reducing overall acceptance.

Secondly, general attitudes towards nuclear power as expressed by the rejection of the 'exit' proposition no longer explain why individuals accept an unfavourable siting decision. It seems as though the introduc-tion of financial compensation serves to supersede the content of the original social problem. This, of course, is related to our third proposi-tion stating that the effects of motivation crowding-out are more severe if individuals believe that social decisions must be taken on the basis of content.

III LIMITS TO COMPENSATION

The conclusions for siting policies are straightforward:

(1) It is not possible to add a monetary compensation to a relatively well-accepted siting scheme without the risk of jeopardizing much of the support rallied by a carefully designed siting procedure. This result is supported by other research: Kunreuther and Easterling (1990) find that increased tax rebates do not elicit an increased willingness to accept a nuclear waste facility in Nevada. They explicitly reject the possibility that the rebates offered were simply too small. Similar results are reported for nuclear waste repositories in other parts of the United States (see, for example, Carnes *et al.*, 1983).

(2) The heavier the support for a noxious facility depending on the perceived fairness of burden sharing, the greater the damage caused by monetary incentives. There is a clear trade-off between the

possibility of mustering support for a noxious facility by activating people's sense of civic duty, and the efficiency of using price incentives.

(3)   As our econometric analysis shows, people are clearly not irrational in their responses to siting announcements. Factors such as risk, detrimental economic effects, diminished property values, as well as wider political considerations are what cause people to oppose siting plans. This opens the way to winning additional support by reducing the disamenities associated with noxious facilities. Risk mitigation in particular will contribute to overcoming local resistance. People expect developers to offer technically optimal solutions. Since citizens react in a rational way to siting announcements, it is tempting – at least for economists – to offer monetary compensation for whatever risk a facility might still represent. However, by doing so, the developer precisely forgoes the support of those most interested in technically and socially sound solutions. If this group suspects the facility will not serve the real long-term interests of their region or nation and that money is used to cover up this fact, they react by withdrawing their intrinsically motivated support.

This outcome is of general relevance for both economic theory and policy. It identifies a particular limit of monetary compensation to rally support for a socially desired enterprise. While this does not question the Relative Price Effect of monetary compensation in any way, this measure becomes less effective. With high dead weight cost of taxation, this policy instrument may even become inefficient.

NOTES

1.   O'Hare (1977) was among the first to suggest the use of monetary compensation as a means to overcome the siting problem. Since then, a rather large literature has evolved. Among many others, the search in the US for locations for noxious facilities in general, and nuclear waste repositories in particular is discussed by Downey (1985), Hamilton (1993), Kunreuther and Easterling (1990), Mitchell and Carson (1986), O'Hare, *et al.* (1983), Opaluch, *et al.* (1993), Sigmon (1987), and Slovic, *et al.* (1991). Goetze (1982), Kunreuther and Portney (1991), and O'Sullivan (1993) contain theoretical considerations. Kemp (1992), Linnerooth-Bayer, *et al.* (1994), Oberholzer-Gee, *et al.* (1995), Renn, *et al.* (1996), and Vari, *et al.* (1993) present European case studies and international comparisons.

2.   When we conducted the survey it was suspected that the town of Wolfenschiessen in Central Switzerland would be chosen as the final site. To lend the survey as much

credibility as possible, 225 of the 305 interviews were made in Wolfenschiessen. Upon completion of the survey, the agency ultimately recommended Wolfenschiessen indeed.

3. $2[LL(N)-LL(0)] = 207.801$ with 9 degrees of freedom, Chi-Sq p-value = 0.000.

4. For a general discussion of odds ratios, see Hensher and Johnson (1981) or Hosmer and Lemeshow (1989). In a logistic regression model $\beta_1 = g(x+1) - g(x)$, the slope coefficient represents the change in the logit for a change of one unit in the independent variable x. With a dichotomous independent variable $x - 1$, the odds of the outcome being present (that is, the repository is accepted) is defined as $\pi(1)/[1 - \pi(1)]$. The odds of the outcome being present with $x = 0$ is given by $\pi(0)/[1 - \pi(0)]$. The odds ratio ψ is defined as the ratio of the odds for $x = 1$ to the odds for $x = 0$. Therefore

$$\psi = \frac{\pi(1)/[1-\pi(1)]}{\pi(0)/[1-\pi(0)]}$$

The estimated coefficients reported in the table represent the log of the odds ratio

$$ln(\psi) = ln\left[\frac{\pi(1)/[1-\pi(1)]}{\pi(0)/[1-\pi(0)]}\right] = g(1) - g(0)$$

which is called the logit difference. For logistic regression with a dichotomous independent variable

$$\psi = e^{\beta_1}$$

and the logit difference is

$$ln(\psi) = ln(e^{\beta_1}) = \beta_1$$

5. They give the procedure at least 4 points on a scale from '1 = not acceptable at all' to '6 = completely acceptable'.

6. The compensation offered here is quite substantial. Median household income for our respondents is CHF 5250 per month.

7. Acceptance rates are 24.3 per cent when CHF 2500 is offered, 24.8 per cent with CHF 5000, and 24.7 per cent with CHF 7500.

8. $2[LL(N)-LL(0)] = 36.714$ with 9 degrees of freedom, Chi-Sq p-value = 0.000.

SUGGESTED FURTHER READINGS

The major problems connected with the NIMBY-problems are discussed in
Easterling, Douglas and Howard Kunreuther (1995), *The Dilemma of Siting a High-Level Nuclear Waste Repository*, Boston: Kluwer.
Portney, Kent E. (1991), *Siting Hazardous Waste Treatment Facilities: The NIMBY Syndrome*, New York: Auburn House.
The situation in the United States and in Canada is discussed in
Rabe, Barry G. (1994), *Beyond NIMBY: Hazardous Waste Siting in Canada and the United States*, Washington, DC: Brookings Institution.
The use of the price system for finding a site is suggested, for instance in

Kunreuther, Howard and Paul R. Kleindorfer (1986), 'A Sealed-Bid Auction
    Mechanism for Siting Noxious Facilities', *American Economic Review, Pa-
    pers and Proceedings*, **76** (May), 295–9.
A more extended analysis of Crowding Theory in the NIMBY-context is pro-
vided in
Frey, Bruno S., Felix Oberholzer-Gee and Reiner Eichenberger (1997), 'The
    Old Lady Visits Your Backyard: A Tale of Morals and Markets', *Journal of
    Political Economy*, **104**, 193–209.

9. Social and organizational policy

Crowding-Out Effects, and their relationship to the Price Effect, are of crucial importance in many policy areas. Here some additional applications are provided in selected policy areas.

I REGULATORY POLICY

Managers of a firm who care for the health and welfare of their employees for intrinsic reasons, introduce accident precaution measures beyond what is required by law. They will, however, to some extent reduce their internal motivation when such measures are externally imposed by law. Such behaviour has indeed been empirically observed for regulations in the area of occupational health and safety in the United States: '... when they [the managers, BSF] felt they acted responsibly, some business managers respond by taking the position that they will act no more responsibly than the agency's rules require' (Bardach and Kagan, 1982, p. 107; also Veljanovski, 1984). The change induced by imposing the social regulations has proved to be smaller than predicted because the firms affected who did more than required reduce their effort to the minimum required. The managers' intrinsic motivation has been crowded out.

In contrast, when the managers' efforts to do more than required from a legal and profit-maximizing point of view is duly acknowledged by the regulators, the managers maintain their beneficent policy. However, continually indulging in intrinsic motivation is only possible if the markets for the goods produced, for the ownership of the firm, and for managers are not fully competitive.[1] Private firms in state welfare countries, such as Scandinavia, are unlikely to do better than requested by the government regulations because the private sector's intrinsically motivated 'demand' for social policy has been taken over by the government.

This proposition is consistent with empirical observations. An example is volunteer work. Voluntary social activities must be expected to be lower in state welfare countries, an effect which has indeed been found in econometric analyses of the supply of volunteer labour (Menchik and Weisbrod, 1987, p. 135). A study group has found that 'voluntary work has traditionally been viewed in a negative light in Sweden and that the activities of voluntary care organizations are of modest proportions by the standards of many other countries' (Lågergren and Lund, 1984, pp. 210, 212). In the Swedish setting, this study group put no faith in intrinsic motivations but rather they 'believe that a compulsory social service will be needed to provide [...] the care and welfare services needed' (p. 211). This implicitly recognizes that the government intervention of the extent and intensity typical for Sweden has crowded out intrinsic motivation, and that compulsion has to be used instead. On the other hand, in countries such as Germany or Switzerland where the state interferes less with the social aspect of the economy than in Scandinavia (see, for example, Dixon and Scheurell, 1989), one would expect to see a larger extent of intrinsically motivated social activities. This is again supported by both circumstantial evidence (in such countries voluntary social organizations are thriving) as well as by scientific research (Weisbrod, 1988 gives extensive references).

II   CRIME PREVENTION

The economics of crime (Becker, 1968; Tullock, 1974) rests on the Price or Deterrence Effect: when the cost of committing a crime is increased relative to legal activities, the extent of crime is reduced. On the other hand, there is a great deal of evidence that intrinsic motivation in the form of moral convictions is of crucial importance for people's behaviour in this area. Indeed, most sociologists, psychologists and criminologists concentrate exclusively on internal values with respect to crime, thus (implicitly) assuming that intrinsic factors have a systematic and strong effect on criminal behaviour. Grasmick and Bursik (1990) find that when intrinsic motivation is introduced as a determinant of crime in addition to deterrence within a standard subjective expected utility maximizing model, behaviour is better explained. For the three crime areas they study, there is strong evidence that the shame of violating one's intrinsic beliefs contributes to forsaking criminal activities, highlighting 'the importance of internal control in producing conformity to the law' (p. 840).

When individuals' behaviour is more tightly monitored in order to raise the probability of apprehension, and if punishment is increased, actors observe the laws more strictly because of the higher expected cost of crime, and not because they are intrinsically motivated to behave morally. Due to the 'overjustification' effect produced, it is to be expected that the individuals, who, on average, then have a lower intrinsic motivation to obey the law, would exploit the possibilities allowed by the law more fully. For example, when maximum speed limits are starkly reduced, individuals observe them to the extent they find optimal in view of the expected punishment. At the same time, they tend to go to the limit wherever it suits them because they are morally less inhibited (for instance, curves are taken at the maximum speed, which previously were not). If the damaging effect on the intrinsic motivation to drive carefully is sufficiently strong, reducing the speed limit may lead to an unintended, perverse result, that is, more and not fewer accidents happen. There is an analogy to Peltzman's (1975) perverse effect of introducing the obligatory use of safety belts.[2] In this case, the increase in accidents is due to the fact that the drivers compensate the risk reduction (effected by wearing safety belts) by driving more recklessly. The imposition of air-bags in cars has also induced people to drive more aggressively so that the risk of death has increased for other traffic participants (Peterson *et al.*, 1995). This is a special case of our more general substitution effect.

A perverse effect of increasing punishment has also been identified by Akerlof and Dickens (1982), and Dickens (1986). Their argument is based on a specific psychological theory – cognitive dissonance. According to that psychological theory, individuals endeavour to make their convictions and motivations on the one hand, and their behaviour on the other hand, compatible with each other (Festinger, 1957). Akerlof and Dickens argue that when punishment is low and behaviour conforms to law, individuals build up a motivation to obey the law. With high punishment, on the other hand, no such build-up is needed to obey the law. There is, therefore, no restraint once the punishment is removed. Hence, higher sanctions may increase crime, a proposition for which some empirical evidence is adduced. Akerlof and Dickens' model may again be considered a special case of the more general model used here. The major difference is that the effect of cognitive dissonance only becomes relevant for behaviour when punishment is removed. Our approach allows for direct, as well as for positive and negative impacts on intrinsic motivation and, *ceteris paribus*, on behaviour. The Crowding Effect depends on how an individual's perceived self-determination is affected, and on whether the external intervention is conceived by the individual to acknowledge or reject the exercise of intrinsic motivation. According to the Crowding-Out Effect, a rise in expected punishment shifts the locus of control to other persons or institutions and tends to reduce the effectiveness of deterrence. In contrast, there are circumstances in which intrinsic motivation, and with that, the effectiveness of punishment, is supported. A relevant case is when increased monitoring does not only serve to catch delinquents but also serves to acknowledge the moral behaviour of those not violating the law.

III BLOOD DONATION

The readiness to donate blood is another area where Crowding-Out Effects induced by monetary rewards help to explain empirical observations which are difficult or even impossible to explain otherwise. Four issues will be discussed.

1 Extent of commercial blood market

Standard economic theory 'suggests that donors *would* respond to prices by supplying more than they do at zero price' (Cooper and Culyer, 1973, p. 131; Roberts and Wolkoff, 1988). Titmuss in his book *The Gift Relationship* (1970), on the other hand, claimed that to pay donors for giving blood may discourage cherished values. When Solow (1971) and Arrow (1972), discussed this proposition they assumed that the effects of price incentives can simply be added to that of altruistic donations, as the two motivations are independent of each other. As a result, they predicted that a price increase in the commercial market for blood raises the total quantity supplied (both free of charge and at a price).

Many people have a strong aversion against commercializing blood donation. 'Selling blood is regarded as an act unworthy of a respectable citizen', and there exists 'outrage at the mere idea of "selling blood" for money' (Ireland and Koch, 1973, pp. 148 and 151). A survey among American donors and non-donors reveals that 'a large majority of (the) respondents had a very negative attitude toward the purchase of blood from donors' (Drake *et al.*, 1982, p. 108). Empirical studies have found moral considerations to be of great importance for voluntary donors (for instance, Oswalt, 1977; Lightman, 1981). Blood donation is considered to be the most convincing example of true altruism and a primordial example of commitment (Collard, 1978, p. 5; see also Sen,

1982, 1987). Individuals who give blood for altruistic reasons suffer a utility loss when blood is priced. Intrinsic motivation is crowded out and spills over to the blood donation sector in which no pricing is applied. There, the intrinsic motivation of people who have so far donated gratis is reduced. It is predicted that introducing or increasing the commercial blood market price raises the quantity supplied due to the monetary incentives, but decreases the quantity supplied free of charge. Due to the difficulty in isolating the many different influences on blood supply, there do not seem to be any reliable real-life observations on whether, or to what extent, pricing blood discourages unpaid donations: 'The limited empirical evidence available in that context is ambiguous' (Hansmann, 1987, p. 68). Whether the total blood supply falls depends on the relative size of the Price and of the Crowding-Out Effect. In a country where most of the blood is supplied gratis, paying for blood is likely to reduce total supply.

An experiment conducted with students suggests that an increase in the price offered for blood at a low price level decreases the quantity supplied and increases it only when the price is further raised (Ireland and Koch, 1973, pp. 152–4). This is perfectly consistent with Crowding Theory: as long as there still exists an intrinsic motivation, the Crowding-Out Effect prevails, but once it is totally destroyed, the standard reaction takes over. Another experiment yielded the same outcome: in a group regularly donating blood without monetary compensation, the offer of payment significantly reduced donation rates compared to a control group not offered payment (Upton, 1973).

On the basis of Titmuss' (1970) book, one would be led to think that the commercial supply of blood in the United States is of great importance. This was true at the time that book was written. Between 1965 and 1967, 80 per cent of all blood was obtained from paid donors. Since 1973, a 'National Blood Policy' by the Department of Health, Education, and Welfare, officially undertaken to improve the quality of blood donated (see, for example, Wallace, 1985), has reduced the commercial share of blood donation drastically and today 'virtually all whole blood is obtained from unpaid donors' (Hansmann, 1987, p. 60; Drake *et al.*, 1982, pp. 4–7, indicate a share of 3–4 per cent paid donors). Between 1971 and 1980, whole blood collected from volunteers rose by 39 per cent, while that from paid donors fell by 76 per cent (see also Hough, 1978, table 1, p. 102). Thus, to some extent at least, when the use of pricing is discontinued, an intrinsic motivation to donate blood for free re-emerges.

Standard neo-classical economics deals with the very small commercial share of the market only, and the question arises of what economics can say about the unpaid part of the supply of blood that is by far larger. In favour of the standard theory, it may be argued that what matters is the *marginal* blood contribution which, in the United States and other countries, is paid for. The evidence shows, however, that precisely in emergencies (for instance, when natural catastrophes or wars occur) blood donated gratis strongly increases (Baumol and Oates, 1979, p. 297). Here, one draws on a type of intrinsic (altruistic) motivation aroused under special circumstances rather than on marginal effects produced by the Price Effect.

2 Non-monetary inducements to voluntary donors

Noting the small share of the commercial blood market, even in the United States, adherents of standard economic theory tend to extend the definition of a 'price' also to include non-monetary but material inducements. They argue that there are fewer voluntary contributions than there appear to be because donors actually receive a non-monetary form of compensation for giving blood.

Crowding Theory offers a different interpretation of the non-monetary inducements offered. It is not a price in the usual sense but a *signal* indicating the appreciation of, or acknowledgement for, the voluntary contribution. This particular form of 'compensation' increases the marginal benefit of giving for intrinsic reasons, supporting the altruistic motivation for donating it free. It is hypothesized that the administrators of such inducement make a considerable effort to distinguish it from a normal price; in particular, the inducement is given in non-tradeable forms.

Empirical evidence supports Crowding Theory. In both Europe and America, the non-monetary compensation which is widely used (Ireland and Koch, 1973, p. 149) is given in the form of a free fruit juice and a sandwich, both non-tradeable goods of little value. Standard economics offers no explanation of why simpler monetary rewards are not used as an inducement, instead of juice and sandwiches. In contrast, our theory acknowledges the basic difference between an incentive payment and a (material) signal of recognition.

3 Size of the blood market between countries

The extent of blood commercialization varies significantly between countries. To explain these differences, Crowding Theory focuses on the extent to which explicit markets are accepted as legitimate resource allocation mechanisms in different countries and cultures. It is acknowledged that a given payment offers a larger incentive to donate blood in poorer than in richer countries. As pointed out earlier in Chapter 3, Americans seem to be more ready to accept the use of prices than Europeans. As a consequence, in the United States, crowding out of intrinsic motivation by pricing is expected to be weaker than in Europe. It is therefore more efficient for blood-collecting organizations to use pricing for blood in the United States than in Europe. The empirical facts are again consistent with this prediction. The commercial blood market in the United States is larger than in the United Kingdom and elsewhere in Europe or in Japan (Institute of Economic Affairs, 1973; Eckert, 1985, p. 13).

4 Market separation

In line with other economists, Arrow (1975, p. 19) wonders '*why* it be that the creation of a [commercial] market for blood would decrease the altruism embodied in giving blood'. Accordingly, there is no need to separate supply between donated and paid blood. Crowding Theory, on the other hand, takes into account that (under identifiable conditions) the motivation to donate blood spills over from one sector to another. Blood presents a good example for a motivation spill-over because the same good is involved but is given in sectors with and without pricing.

Again, empirical evidence is consistent with our theory. The blood market *is* neatly separated. 'If there is one universal tendency, it is toward assigning one organization exclusive authority to collect blood within a defined territory' (Drake *et al.*, 1982, p. 120). In the United States, for example, the Red Cross and the American Association of Blood Banks (AABB) collect blood without paying the donors, while commercial blood banks do. Those intrinsically motivated donors and those doing it for money are thus separated as far as possible.

IV MILITARY ORGANIZATION

Crowding Theory also throws light on the choice between forms of organization, in particular between a voluntary (paid) and a conscripted military service. The large body of economic literature on the issue[3] does not discuss the incentives to fight under the two institutional arrangements. While the different quality (education) of a volunteer as opposed to a conscripted army are considered, the fighting morale or intrinsic motivation are (implicitly) taken as given. Yet the experience of the last two (major) wars the United States was engaged in suggests that the choice between coercion and voluntarism strongly affects the efficiency of an army. Discipline and fighting morale in the conscripted American army which lost the Vietnam war was low, while it was high in the voluntary army which successfully fought the war in the Gulf.[4] This impression is shared by military scholars. The British military strategist and historian Liddell Hart (1982, p. 35–6) flatly states: 'Twenty-five years spent in the study of war [...] brought me to see that the compulsory principle was fundamentally inefficient', and he attributes it to intrinsic motivation: 'Efficiency springs from enthusiasm [...] enthusiasm is incompatible with compulsion.' The most successful sections of the German military forces in World War II – the air force and tank force – were recruited on a semi-voluntary basis. The conscripted, ordinary German army did not have 'anything like the same enthusiasm [...] which constituted a basic weakness in Germany's apparent strength' (Liddell Hart, 1982, pp. 36–7; see in general, Kellet, 1982; Richardson, 1978).

These empirical observations go well with Crowding Theory. The more coercive military enlistment is, the more strongly self-determination is reduced, undermining the intrinsic motivation to fight. A voluntary army, on the other hand, is based on choice, does not affect self-determination and therefore does not damage the fighting spirit. Taking into account the effect of organizational form on intrinsic motivation also allows us to explain observations relating to different variants of the draft. A general conscription where all able men serve (as, for example, in Switzerland) is less damaging to intrinsic motivation than a lottery (as was, for instance, applied in the United States) because: 'The man drafted on the basis of a lottery is a loser' (Janowitz, 1973, p. 74) and: 'Under a lottery system ... the military system is considered a form of punishment [and] morale [is] more difficult to maintain' (Hayes, 1967, p. 18). The draft lottery thus gives young men a clear signal that the government does not care for a citizens' intrinsic motivation to serve the country, inducing them to reduce morale.

Our analysis also suggests that to allow conscripts to buy their way out for a fee, or to provide a replacement as a 'means to increase the efficiency in a conscription system' (Ross, 1988, p. 15) is ill conceived because it is bound to undermine the intrinsic motivation of those remaining in the army. During the American Civil War, both the Union and the Confederation allowed this form of evasion, with such dire consequences to both sides that the experiment was given up (Billings, 1971; Ross, 1988).

NOTES

1. An exception is when such policies raise the employees' productivity, in which case it can subsist also under perfect competition. For experimental evidence of a related proposition, see Fehr, Kirchsteiger and Riedl (1993).
2. The empirical evidence has been disputed, for example, Crandall and Graham (1984) find a modest beneficial effect. However, it has been observed far beyond driving that regulations are little, or not at all, effective. See, for instance, for consumer protection, occupational safety, health and pharmaceutical prescriptions, Magat and Viscusi (1990), Viscusi (1984).
3. See Anderson's (1976) bibliography, and the collection of articles by Tax (1967) and Anderson (1982). A more recent contribution is Ross (1988).
4. Lieut. General John H. Yeosack, commander of the army units in the Gulf said 'I have fewer disciplinary problems commanding a third of a million troops now than I did in 1973 commanding 1,000 men' (*Time*, March 18, 1991, p. 25). See also Gary Becker's column on the volunteer army (*Business Week*, March 25, 1991, p. 14) espousing the same view.

SUGGESTED FURTHER READINGS

Various types of regulatory policy and the respective reactions of firms to it are discussed in
Bardach, Eugene and Robert A. Kagan (1982), *Going by the Book: The Problem of Regulatory Unreasonableness*, Philadelphia: Temple University.
Crime is analysed from the economic point of view in
Auerbach, Alan J. (ed.) (1996), 'Symposia – The Economics of Crime', *The Journal of Economic Perspectives*, **10** (1), 3–65.
and from a general social science view in
Grasmick, Harold G. and Robert J. Bursik (1990), 'Conscience, Significant Others, and Rational Choice: Extending the Deterrence Model', *Law and Society Review*, **24**, 837–61.
The discussion on blood donation has been much influenced by
Titmuss, Richard M. (1970), *The Gift Relationship*, London: Allen and Unwin.
The traditional economic position is developed in
Arrow, Kenneth J. (1974), 'Gifts and Exchanges', *Philosophy and Public Affairs*, **1**, 343–62.
The organization of the military is treated in
Anderson, Martin (ed.) (1982), *The Military Draft. Selected Readings on Conscription*, Stanford: Hoover Institution.

10. Work motivation and compensation policy

The principal–agent paradigm and the closely related theory of contracts, property rights and organization theory, as well as modern institutional economics in general have without doubt provided major insights into industrial relations. These theories have, however, been exclusively concerned with *extrinsic* work motivation. Indeed, economists assume that people would not work if they were not compensated (Lane, 1991, p. 349). Already the Romans knew better: '*labor ipse voluptas*', that is, work in itself conveys pleasure. This assumption is inconsistent with the extensive amount of volunteer work. On the other hand, people without employment are often deeply depressed, and their life – which centres around work – loses its purpose (Darity and Goldsmith, 1996).

Principal–agent theorists may well argue that these counter arguments are irrelevant for their analysis. When people work for *intrinsic* reasons, the supply curve of labour is simply shifted rightward as an exogenously given constant amount of work is added. The workers' marginal decisions with respect to work performance are unaffected. Instead, the principal–agent paradigm concentrates on the incentives to bring forth a desired amount and intensity of work (for instance, Sappington, 1991). A widespread use of individual incentive payments is advised where the financial compensation is contingent on work performance (for example, Stiglitz, 1987). Following the traditional view of people as selfish utility maximizers, it is expected that every worker always tries to do as little as possible as he or she benefits from avoiding or shirking work. In Williamson's (1975) concept of 'opportunism', workers are even taken to make an active effort to minimize work. The tendency for shirking is more prevalent in teams of workers because of the public good nature of collective output, and shirking is expected to be even more widespread.

Principal–agent theory sees industrial relations to be dominated by distrust, and in particular, by workers' shirking.[1] As a result, the analysis focuses almost obsessively on the principals' need to monitor and control the agents (workers). Monitoring should be accompanied by negative sanctions, in particular the threat of dismissal, unemployment thus being a 'discipline device' (Shapiro and Stiglitz, 1984) as well as by rewards such as financial incentives, or 'efficiency wages' (Akerlof and Yellen, 1986).

Payments contingent on performance are a much discussed means to raise worker productivity but in reality they often turn out to be more a declaration than actual firm policy (Nalbantian, 1987). A careful meta-analysis of many hundreds of studies of implemented incentive wages (Guzzo and Katzell, 1987) leads to two conclusions: (i) as economists expect, financial incentives work and raise productivity on average; and (ii) there is such a large variance of outcomes that this effect is not statistically significant. In many cases, a positive effect on productivity is noted, but in a number of cases it is zero or even negative. The empirical picture is thus inconsistent with the presumption of principal–agency theory that incentive payments unequivocally raise worker productivity.

In view of the fact that the empirical situation is unclear, it is helpful to consider what contribution Crowding-Out Theory is able to make. The task is to find out under what economically relevant conditions an external intervention by the principal reduces agents' work morale, and when that link can safely be left out. At the same time, it is to be analysed in what work situations intrinsically motivated employees perform better, and when it is preferable to apply extrinsic incentives, in particular financial rewards. Once we know more, the mixed empirical picture revealed may be accounted for.[2] In addition, aspects of organizational behaviour which seem puzzling from the point of view of traditional theory (see Stiglitz, 1987) may be explained. One is the fact that incentive payments are more frequently used for managers and low level workers, but less so for the large number of middle-level employees, or another that bondage of agents is 'virtually never' observed in reality (Baker, *et al.*, 1988, p. 613), or that there are presently strong efforts to flatten organizational hierarchy, as well as the current trend to participatory or consultative management.

Section I sets the concepts of intrinsic and extrinsic motivation into the perspective of work. The conditions for external intervention crowding-out (and sometimes crowding-in) intrinsic work motivation are the subject of section II. The following section III presents empirical evidence on the propositions advanced. Section IV considers the consequences for work performance, and section V concludes the chapter.

I INTRINSIC AND EXTRINSIC WORK MOTIVATION

Table 10.1 shows the relationship between intrinsic and extrinsic incentives in the work context. For simplicity, only a high and a low level of the two types of motivation are differentiated. In reality, there is, of course, a continuum.

Table 10.1   Work performance induced by intrinsic and extrinsic motivation

		Intrinsic Motivation	
		low (absent)	high
External intervention	weak (absent)	(1) missing work incentives	(3) work morale
		(B) ——————→	
	strong	(2) extrinsic work incentives	(4) oversufficient work justification
		(A) ←————— (C) ——————→	

Principal–agent theory vertically compares (1) and (2) where intrinsic work motivation can be disregarded. It studies how work performance can be affected by manipulating external intervention. It shows in particular the conditions under which a particular wage scheme raises workers' effort and productivity. Crowding Theory horizontally compares cells (1) and (3), and (2) and (4). Cell (3) indicates those activities where individuals are solely induced by their inner motivation to perform. Cell (4) combines high intrinsic and extrinsic work incentives; the respective persons are doubly motivated to perform.

The arrows in Table 10.1 indicate that motivational combinations are unstable. Most importantly, and of foremost relevance for industrial economics, the combined existence of both intrinsic and extrinsic incentives may lead to 'over-sufficient work justification', inducing people to reduce their intrinsic motivation.[3] This is shown by arrow (A) leading from cell (4) to cell (2). On the other hand, when no work incentives exist (cell (1)), there are cases where persons start to like the activity so that they then perform it for intrinsic reasons (arrow (B) leading from cell (1) to cell (3)).

1 Crowding-out work morale
When a work activity is supported by both high work morale and external intervention, a psychologically unstable situation arises. The agent is 'over motivated' as she would do the work even if one motivation was reduced or absent. A rational actor responds by reducing that motivation which is under her control, that is, she lowers her intrinsic work motivation.

2 Crowding-in work morale
People who are insufficiently motivated when performing an activity look for a justification why they do the job. It is possible that after some time they start to enjoy their job, and become intrinsically motivated. Most parents know this effect: if they can make their children undertake an activity without forcing them, it quite often happens that the children start to enjoy it. This build-up of motivation represents the movement from cell (1) to cell (3) in Table 10.1, indicated by the arrow (B). The strict work-for-pay orientation towards work is given up provided intrinsic rewards are perceived and are attainable. In that case, intrinsic rewards undermine the importance of extrinsic rewards (see Gruenberg, 1980). While these 'hidden gains of inadequate rewards' (Lane, 1991, p. 379) work in the opposite direction of the 'hidden costs of reward', they are not simply symmetrical. The process of building up work morale is as a rule much slower than destroying it, and is less reliable. In many cases, persons insufficiently justified to perform a task simply stop doing it. The conditions under which a virtuous process of rising intrinsic work motivation sets in are not known so far.

A second Crowding-In Effect is based on a quite different psychological mechanism. An external intervention may raise intrinsic work motivation when people regard this action as acknowledging their high work morale. This movement is indicated in Table 10.1 by arrow (C) leading from cell (2) to cell (4). Work remuneration perceived as fair supports work morale.

This chapter concentrates on crowding-out work morale because it is more relevant for the problems of principal–agency theory: the possibility of controlling agents by external intervention is questioned. One of the bases of that theory, and of neo-classical economics generally, is put into doubt. However, the Crowding-In Effect is not altogether uninteresting for principal–agency theory because – as will be argued later – it is not always desirable to have agents motivated by higher work morale.

II CONDITIONS FOR CROWDING-OUT WORK MORALE

Considering Table 10.1, it can be seen that there are two requirements for work morale to be crowded out by external interventions: (1) the agent must have a (sufficiently) high intrinsic work motivation at the outset; and (2) a crowding-out process must take place. These two requirements will now be discussed in turn.

1 High work morale
Persons can have a high intrinsic work motivation for many different reasons. The following three are of particular interest because they may be influenced by appropriate measures.

(a) An *interesting* task for the agents supports their intrinsic motivation to perform well. The evaluation of which tasks and occupations are 'interesting' and which are 'dull' varies considerably between individuals. However, it seems fair to state that people in liberal and academic professions tend to consider their jobs intrinsically more interesting than those of less educated employees.

Manual workers generally have low intrinsic work motivation; they essentially are in a firm because they need the monetary income to survive (see, for example, Goldthorp *et al.*, 1968; Kornhauser, 1965; Lane, 1991, ch. 18). However, when their income rises above the (culturally defined) subsistence level, they seek meaning in work. Today, a general increase in intrinsic satisfaction with work has been observed (Mortimer, 1979; Yankelovich and Immerwahr, 1984), and has been related to 'post-materialism' (Inglehart, 1981). Professions with internalized standards of excellence – which is a type of 'achievement motivation' (McClelland, 1961) – have in general a higher work motivation based on feelings of competence and self-determination. Indeed, as scientists and artists are considered to have a significant level of intrinsic work motivation,[4] they are therefore less closely supervised (for example, Osterman, 1994).

(b) *Personal* relationships between principal and agent support intrinsic work motivation. In a situation of perfect competition, the relationship between individuals is totally guided by the price, and there is in principle anonymity between the trading partners. As soon as one moves outside the perfect market, personal interactions become important as well as the role of intrinsic work motivation. This is obvious for decision-making systems centred on bargaining where the actors necessarily enter into social interactions.

(c) When the agents are able to *participate* in the decisions taken by the principal, work morale tends to be high. It is this relationship which lies at the heart of the arguments for co-determination, but also for flatter hierarchy within conventional firms. In Japanese firms relying on consensus processes and collaboration among employees, workers have higher work morale and more commitment to their firm than in comparable American firms relying more on hierarchical decision-making (Aoki, 1990). In an econometric cross-section study, Gordon (1994) finds that the smaller the intensity of supervision, the higher the workers' bargaining power and factual co-determination. This is consistent with the existence of a large Crowding-Out Effect and a corresponding rational reaction by the principals, namely to discipline workers less.

2 Negative effect on work morale

Crowding-Out Effects take place – as has been established above – when an external intervention is perceived to be *controlling*. In contrast, when the intervention by the principal is understood to be *supportive*, intrinsic work motivation is unaffected or may possibly even rise. Whether the principal's intervention crowds out intrinsic work motivation thus depends on the employees' perception. This perception is not haphazard but may be linked to economically relevant determinants.

Two conditions may be identified which systematically influence the way external interventions are perceived by employees.

(a)   When employees get rewarded only if they have performed exactly according to their chief's directions, their intrinsic work motivation is negatively affected. The more a reward is contingent on the performance desired by the principal, the more strongly the locus of control is shifted from intrinsic to extrinsic incentives, and the more work morale is crowded out.

A monetary payment received through the functioning of the market constitutes a case where the reward depends on performance; in a perfectly competitive market the reward (wage rate) depends exactly on the marginal product performed. The price system therefore tends to substitute intrinsic with extrinsic motivation. On the other hand, a market reward may also indicate competence and then tends to raise work morale. 'Scientists, artists and entrepreneurs receive rewards for performance that may be described as feelings of competence and self-determination' (Lane, 1991, p. 389), an aspect which has been emphasized by Schumpeter (1936).

Within the bureaucracy of a firm or other organization, the effect of reward contingency depends very much on the context and the way rewards are being applied. Four cases may be distinguished:

(i)   In firms, managers spend a great deal of time establishing personal relationships with their inferiors (see, for example, Mintzberg, 1975). This activity serves to build up intrinsic motivation, but as a consequence, an external intervention perceived to be controlling may crowd out the intrinsic motivation fostered. This danger is understood by top management. As a consequence, monetary incentive payments are little used in reality although standard economics strongly favours them (see for example Baker, Jensen and Murphy, 1988).

(ii)   *Promotion* based on performance, if interpreted as an acknowledgement of general competence, tends to raise work morale. However, if perceived as a reward contingent only on one's specific externally determined performance, this tends to reduce it. This does not mean that in the latter case the promoted person is less motivated overall, but only that his or her intrinsic motivation has been marginally substituted by the external incentive of promotion. It therefore does not contradict the basic incentive-promoting assumption underlying the economics of tournaments (see Lazear and Rosen, 1981), provided the additional external motivation is larger than the crowding out effect.

(iii) *Honours and Prizes* given contingent on a particular performance (for instance, the nomination to 'employee of the month', see Kohn, 1993a; 1993b) tend negatively to affect intrinsic motivation, as these extrinsic factors will take its place instead. This being understood, a lot of trouble is taken *not* to grant these rewards as a response to a particular performance, but rather as a recognition of a person's dedication to his or her work or career in general. Titles, orders and other honours (such as honorary doctorates) are normally given for one's lifelong work, and are thus perceived by the recipients as a recognition of their competence, raising intrinsic motivation.

(iv) The *monetization* of rewards tends to emphasize performance contingency because agents are used to establish a relationship between the size of the income received and their performance. Non-monetary gifts in kind (for example, in the form of flowers, books or chocolates) constitute a conscious effort to disassociate the reward from any particular performance. Rather, these gifts are chosen so that the person's self-esteem is acknowledged, thereby bolstering the recipient's intrinsic work motivation. This relationship is understood by firms that increase their employees' attachment not by handing out monetary rewards but rather by giving them gifts in kind.

(b) An employee's perception of whether the principals' intervention is controlling or supporting depends on the extent of differentiation made between the workers. At one extreme, all employees are treated the same by the principal; at the other extreme, the principal makes a conscious effort to distinguish the rewards or commands according to the workers' presumed level of intrinsic motivation. The more uniform the external intervention, the more negatively are those employees affected who have above-average work morale. They therefore adjust their intrinsic motivation downwards. A case in point is the administration of governments and hierarchically structured large private firms which are forced by general rules to intervene uniformly. The public sector, in particular, is often restricted by a general salary scale and finds it difficult or impossible to vary compensation according to the work morale exhibited. As a result, in state-run institutions, more employees reduce their intrinsic work motivation to a low level than is the case in more flexible small private institutions. Intrinsic work motivation tends to be most strongly undermined when the superiors are incapable or unwilling to restrict and punish employees who consciously exploit the system to their personal advantage.

III EMPIRICAL EVIDENCE

The Crowding-Out Effect is not 'pervasive' in all relationships within organizations – as Deci (1978, p. 174) claims. While it is *sometimes* of great importance, and has indeed been disregarded in economic theory, it would be wrong to think that it always occurs in economically relevant settings. Work morale is not even necessarily crowded out when monetary payments are involved. Thus, when rewards are part of a normal contractual relation, they do not crowd out intrinsic motivation. A taxi driver who picks up a passenger from the station (Case 4 in Chapter 2), does not suffer any fall in his work morale, because his work is likely undertaken for monetary profit, or for a purely extrinsic motivation. The situation is quite different if a host picks up his guest from the station.

Crowding-Out Theory for the case of work motivation has been subject to econometric studies. Barkema (1995) looks at firms where the intensity of the personal relationship between the employer and the employees depends on the form of supervision. For the case of managers as agents of a certain firm, one can distinguish three major types: (i) The managers are controlled by the parent company. This corresponds to a rather impersonal relationship. Following our above proposition, a positive influence of monitoring on managers' performance is expected, because intrinsic motivation is little or not at all affected. (ii) The managers are controlled by their firm's chief executive officer and this represents a personalized relationship. According to our proposition, monitoring in this case tends to reduce the agents' effort, as an external intervention shifts the locus of control towards external preferences.

(iii) The managers' behaviour is regulated by the board of directors. The Crowding-Out Effect is, according to our hypothesis, expected to be greater than in case (i) but smaller than in case (ii).

Barkema's data set refers to 116 managers in medium-sized Dutch firms in 1985. They range from between less than one hundred to more than 30,000 employees and cover a wide variety of industries. The managers' individual effort is in line with Holmström and Milgrom (1990) operationalized as the number of hours invested. The intensity of regulating is captured by three aspects: the regularity with which their performance is evaluated; the degree of formality of the evaluation procedure; and the degree to which the managers are evaluated by well-defined criteria. A measurement model is used empirically to establish that these variables meaningfully represent the latent variable 'regulating'. A structural model is then used to show the influence of so-defined external intervention on managers' performance.

The results are consistent with the proposition advanced. The econometrically estimated parameters capturing the effect of external intervention on work performance turns out to be positive and statistically significant in case (i) of impersonal control. In case (ii) of personalized control, on the other hand, the corresponding parameter is statistically significantly negative; regulating strongly crowds out intrinsic motivation, so that the net effect of control on performance is counterproductive. In the intermediate case (iii) of somewhat personalized control, the estimated parameter does not deviate from zero in a statistically significant way, that is, the Price or Disciplinary Effect of the controls is of a similar size as the Crowding-Out Effect.

IV CONSEQUENCES FOR WORK PERFORMANCE

It might be argued that as long as one is not interested in cognitive processes as such, but only in their effect on human behaviour, there is no problem when intrinsic work motivation is substituted by an extrinsic one. It may seem irrelevant what kind of motivation induces people to work as long as they do work.

This view is too simple: the performance induced by intrinsic motivation is not necessarily desirable. There are advantages and disadvantages of having work performed by intrinsically motivated persons.

In some ('humanitarian') circles, self-determination and intrinsic work motivation are considered absolute values to aim for. This view is certainly not shared by those who happen to be in the position of a principal. Self-determined workers may possibly be more content but not necessarily more productive. They may use the discretionary room accorded to them to pursue their own interests (for instance, working at a leisurely pace and only performing those tasks they like) which for the principal is 'shirking'. Hence it is necessary to evaluate the positive and negative consequences of intrinsic work motivation.

Some important *advantages* of intrinsic work motivation are now discussed.[5]

(i) For the agents themselves, work governed by intrinsic motivation is associated with better mental and physical health. Work and life satisfaction are higher than under externally determined work motivation.

(ii) Learning capacity is higher (see Condry and Chambers, 1978). Curiosity is possibly the clearest case of intrinsically rewarding activity, and curiosity leads to creativity and learning. Extrinsic motivation certainly does not exclude learning in the sense of an adaptation by trial and error. Indeed, the price system is an extremely efficient mechanism in this respect as stressed by Hayek (1978), and demonstrated by the much superior performance of market compared to planned economies. Learning due to extrinsic incentives is, however, specific to the situation to which the corresponding rewards or punishments refer, and the incentives cease to work. There exists evidence that 'higher' forms of learning are fostered more by intrinsic than by extrinsic incentives. This applies to double-loop learning (where the new insights are put into the framework of a theory) and even more strongly to deutero-learning (where the new insights are evaluated from the point of view of various theories).[6]

(iii) Similarly to learning, laboratory experiments suggest that cognitively difficult tasks are better solved by intrinsically than extrinsically motivated subjects. A possible explanation is that in undertaking such tasks, there are many setbacks which are better overcome by persons who are thrilled by the task, and less by the rewards that go with an unknown probability of success.

(iv) When the employees have high work morale, the employer saves the cost of disciplining them. Intrinsic motivation is therefore particularly valuable to the employer in areas of high cost monitoring. As a consequence, it may be observed that occupations demanding a high degree of complex and creative problem solving are less intensively supervised than simpler jobs (see, for example, Reber and van Gilder, 1982; Donaldson, 1980). In contrast, persons undertaking work only for the financial rewards restrict their activity strictly to aspects *they* deem relevant to attain the contingent reward (see Kruglanski, 1978, p. 95) – not rarely to the surprise and dismay of the employer who looks at the issue from a different perspective.

Some of important *shortcomings* of having work performed by intrinsically motivated persons are:

(i) from the employers' point of view, employees with high work morale are difficult to guide. Intrinsically motivated workers are, at least to some extent, idiosyncratic, and it often takes a lot of effort and 'psychological feeling' by the principal to get along with them. Exactly because they are intrinsically motivated, a wrong word or two may completely destroy that kind of motivation. The employers are then left with particularly disgruntled employees who may sabotage production. The employers are unable to do much about it because they normally know less about a specific activity than the worker does (basic informational asymmetry). Volunteer work in non-profit institutions is most strongly confronted with this problem. In contrast, when a worker is simply paid to perform a task, the employer may specify precisely the conditions, and does not care how the worker feels.

(ii) It would be wrong to assume that intrinsic motivation is always 'good' and 'socially beneficial'. Historical experience shows that many of the worst crimes in mankind were performed by people who followed inner motives and ideologies. Robespierre and Himmler provide vivid examples that so-motivated persons may create great evil (see also Frey, 1992a, for the case of the treatment of prisoners of war). Not rarely, intrinsically motivated people think of themselves as having a particularly high morale and on that basis are prepared to fight against their own conscience to commit crimes. Thus, in his autobiography, the commandant at Auschwitz Rudolf Hess (1959) who systematically murdered more than 2.5 million persons, claimed that for the greater good of National Socialism he 'stifled all softer emotions'. Passions are moreover often uncontrolled and hazardous (Hirschman, 1982).

(iii) High work morale may be in conflict with equity (Lane, 1991, ch. 20). Intrinsic work satisfaction goes to the worker concerned and cannot be redistributed (at least not directly). Neither can it be directly taxed. Indeed, to the degree that wages are lower for persons intrinsically motivated (that is, in the case of compensating wage differentials induced in a market setting), they are taxed less than persons working for monetary rewards. Empirical evidence (Jencks *et al.*, 1988) suggests that work morale is more unequally distributed than income which exacerbates the equity problem.

(iv) Intrinsic work satisfaction being self-centred, the corresponding utility does not directly benefit society as a whole. In contrast, a voluntary monetary exchange between employers (who pay a wage) and workers (who perform) can be shared by others which under suitable conditions maximizes social welfare (in the sense of Pareto-optimality). It should, however, be added that an intrinsically satisfied employee may indirectly share his welfare by giving a larger portion of his income to his family or friends. However, the transaction costs involved are much higher than on a market, and it is unclear to what extent society as a whole benefits.

V CONCLUSIONS

This chapter endeavours to make both a theoretical and empirical contribution to better understand work. On the theoretical level, it suggests a link between the economics and psychology of work which has so far been disregarded. 'The research ... in those two disciplines has proceeded independently; for the most part there has been little cross referencing involved and few attempts to provide a synthesis of the research findings' (Nalbantian, 1987, p. 8) an evaluation which is shared by a later survey and book (Lazear, 1991, 1995).

On the empirical level, the Crowding Effect may explain some open questions in principal–agent theory as applied to work. One of the unresolved problems (mentioned at the beginning of this chapter) is the fact that incentive wages are used for managers but rarely for middle-level employees (Stiglitz, 1987). This may be explained by noting that managers generally perceive incentive wages as information about their performance while the subordinates perceive it as controlling, so that a condition for crowding-out intrinsic motivation applies. As this is known by the executives of the firm, they do not apply incentive wages at the middle-level to any great extent. Crowding Theory is also consistent with the observation that incentive pay in the form of piece rates is, at least to some extent, used for workers engaged in repetitive activities because typically, they have little, if any, work morale which would be crowded out. On the whole, Crowding Theory may account for the fact that incentive payment is used much less than economists think and propose.

Becker and Stigler (1975) suggest that people looking for work should offer bonds in order to make 'credible commitments' and to improve their chances of being accepted as workers. More generally, bonds can serve to support exchange (Williamson, 1983). However, such bondings have not been observed in reality, not even where the prospective employees have sufficient liquidity to advance this bond (Baker, Jensen and Murphy, 1988, p. 613). Crowding Theory suggests why: when the employer requires a prospective worker to post a bond, he thereby signals massively that he distrusts the employee with the result that the latter's work morale is crowded out. As a consequence, only persons with purely extrinsic motivation would apply for such jobs. The employer foregoes the possibility of hiring persons with intrinsic interest in the tasks to be fulfilled.

Finally, the move towards participatory management is also consistent with Crowding Theory. The increasing role of intrinsic work motivation in economically advanced societies leads firm's executives to make a greater effort to maintain work morale which is better achieved by increasing participation. In hierarchical organizations, in contrast, employees are more induced to shift the locus of control to their superiors, losing intrinsic interest in their work.

More generally, Crowding Theory is consistent with the empirical meta-analysis undertaken by Guzzo and Katzell (1987). They find a positive relationship between incentive wages and performance which is, however, not statistically significant because the variance is extremely wide. This is indeed what Crowding Theory suggests: under some conditions here identified, work morale is unaffected, and productivity increases; under other conditions also identified here, work morale is crowded-out so strongly that productivity does not rise but falls.

NOTES

1. There are certainly exceptions. Thus Sen (1977, p. 101) states that 'to run an organization *entirely* on incentives to personal gain is pretty much a hopeless task' and points to 'commitment and the social relations surrounding it'. Some authors such as Williamson (1975, p. 256) acknowledge the importance of trust and atmosphere as well as 'work for work's sake' but they tend to dismiss these aspects because they are difficult to identify and to model. A different position is taken by Simon (for example, 1991) who argues that elegant formalism should not be sacrificed to relevance. See in general Mayer (1993).
2. Of course, other explanations may also be needed, in particular the group effects induced by financial incentives; see for example, Kendrick (1987).
3. Cell (4) may also be unstable for a purely economic reason. If the principal per-

ceives that an agent performs his or her tasks for intrinsic reasons, the financial compensation will be reduced. The high work morale is compensated (in this case) by a corresponding wage differential. However, agents are in most instances capable of foreseeing that action and will then hide their intrinsic work satisfaction which will become difficult or impossible for the principal to observe and to exploit.

4. This does not mean that artists are *only* intrinsically motivated as the romantic (German) conception of the artist as a genius wants to have it. Even artists with a very high intrinsic motivation are influenced, as everyone else, by monetary payments as may be shown by many examples of famous artists ranging from Michelangelo to Dali. This topic is discussed in the economics of the arts, see, for instance, Frey and Pommerehne (1989).
5. See more fully Lane, 1991, ch. 20 and Congleton, 1991, and with a somewhat different emphasis, de Neubourg and Vendrik, 1994.
6. See Osterloh, Grand and Tiemann (1994), Leibenstein and Maital (1994), based on Argyris and Schön (1978). Experimental evidence is provided in McGraw (1978).

SUGGESTED FURTHER READINGS

Work motivation and compensation issues are discussed from the point of view of principal–agent theory in

Nalbantian, Haig R. (ed.) (1987), *Incentives, Cooperation and Risk Sharing*, Totowa, NJ: Rowman and Zittlefield.

Stiglitz, Joseph E. (ed.) (1991), 'Symposium on Organizations and Economics', *Journal of Economic Perspectives*, **5**, 15–88.

See also

Lazear, Edward P. (1995), *Personnel Economics*, Cambridge, MA: MIT Press.

Psychologists have extensively discussed the Crowding Effect in connection with work, for example.

Notz, W.W. (1975), 'Work Motivation and the Negative Effects of Extrinsic Rewards. A Review of Implications for Theory and Practice', *American Psychologist*, **30**, 884–91.

Enzle, Michael E. and Sharon Anderson (1993), 'Surveillant Intentions and Intrinsic Motivation', *Journal of Psychology and Social Psychology*, **30**, 257–66.

Kohn's book *Punished by Rewards* (quoted at the end of Chapter 2) also contains many examples and references.

Econometric evidence for the Crowding-Out Effect of various types of controls in companies is presented by

Barkema, Harry G.(1995), 'Do Job Executives Work Harder When They Are Monitored?', *Kyklos*, **48**, 19–42.

An extensive analysis of all kinds of pay-for-performance schemes and their effect on productivity is provided in

Blinder, Alan S. (ed.) (1990), *Paying for Productivity. A Look at the Evidence*, Washington, DC: Brookings.

The influence of supervision on work motivation is discussed from the point of view of industrial psychology, for example, by

Reber, Ralph W. and Gloria van Gilder (1982), *Behavioural Insights for Supervision*, Englewood Cliffs, NJ: Prentice Hall.

PART III
Conclusions

11. Consequences for economic policy

The Crowding Effect substantially alters the way policy should be undertaken. The Price Effect, on which orthodox economic policy is based, can no longer be taken always to obtain (section I); an adequate policy should take a broader view, going beyond the area in which a policy instrument is applied (section II); and care should be taken to maintain (and even promote) individuals' desired intrinsic motivation. In many circumstances, policy-makers who want to be effective should use price and regulatory instruments with restraint, or even refrain from intervening (section III). These aspects will now be discussed more fully.

I THE PRICE EFFECT ONLY WORKS SOMETIMES

1 Its role in micro- and macro-policy

The Price Effect – stating that individuals change their behaviour systematically when the cost (or price) of doing so changes – is the backbone of modern economic theory. For that reason, it is also basic for economic policy both at the micro- and macro-economic level.

For policy making at the micro-level, the dependence on the Price Effect is rather obvious. Examples are, for instance, tax incentive programmes for investments which reduce the cost of capital by allowing more rapid depreciation for tax purposes, or subsidy programmes which reduce the cost of hiring additional workers by directly transferring money to the firms. Another example is road pricing where the external effects produced by an individual driver on all other drivers in a congestion are monetarized by imposing an appropriate charge.

The Price Effect is also fundamental for macro-economic policy though it is less visible. In environmental policy, the economic approach is based on the notion that while nature is scarce (that is, carries a positive shadow price), it can be used for free, and is therefore overexploited. Thus, it is necessary to establish a positive price for using natural resources either by directly introducing environmental charges (or taxes), or by handing out licences which because of their scarcity will be traded at a positive price. The increased cost of using the resources provided by nature results in a decrease in demand for its exploitation, and hence contributes to saving the environment. In monetary policy, an increase in the stock of money influences aggregate output and the price level by inducing changes in the relative prices of assets, and also the saving and spending decisions of individuals and firms.

2 The Crowding-Out Effect produces policy differences

According to the Price Effect, policy-makers can always induce an increased supply of an activity (or good) X by raising the supply price p. The supply curve has a positive (or more precisely, non-negative) slope throughout. In Figure 11.1 this supply curve is drawn for simplicity as a straight line. Increasing the price from p_0 to p_B raises the activity level (or quantity supplied) from X_A to X_B. It is worth noting that at a price zero (p_0), orthodox economics allows a positive supply X_A (as drawn in the figure) brought about by what in our terminology is called intrinsic motivation. Orthodox economics is little interested in the question if and why X_A is positive. It maintains the principle that there is little use in speculating about the content of individuals' utility

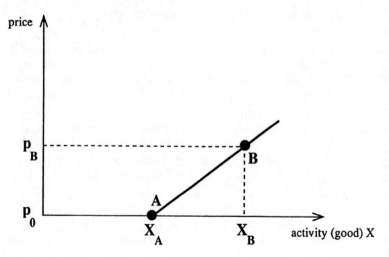

Figure 11.1   The supply curve based on the Price Effect

functions, thus following Stigler and Becker's (1977) famous dictum
'*de gustibus non est disputandum*'.[1]

If crowding-out is allowed, the supply curve takes different forms
depending on the particular way a monetary intervention reduces intrinsic motivation. In Figure 11.2, it is assumed that the Crowding-Out
Effect dominates the Price Effect immediately when the price raises
above zero (or rather when pricing is introduced), but that it does so in
an incremental way. The more the price rises, the stronger is intrinsic
motivation crowded out.

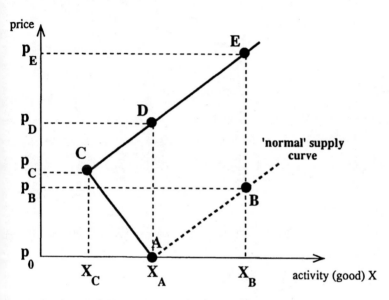

Figure 11.2   The supply curve including a Crowding-Out Effect

A price rise (up to the level p_C) *reduces* the activity from X_A to X_C.
Only when this monetary intervention has crowded out intrinsic motivation completely (at point C) the normal supply curve takes over again as
individuals are then motivated by monetary incentives alone. In order to
raise the supply above the quantity reached before the monetary intervention (X_A), price must be increased above p_D. In order to raise the quantity
above the level which would have been reached in the absence of any
Crowding-Out Effect (X_B), price would have to be kicked above p_E.

The supply curve takes a different shape if the Crowding-Out Effect
only sets in when the price has reached some level, say p_B. At a lower

price, individuals do not perceive the price as controlling (see Chapter 3), or have been accustomed to that level. In that case, the negative slope of the supply curve initiates at point B, and ends at C, as shown in Figure 11.3.

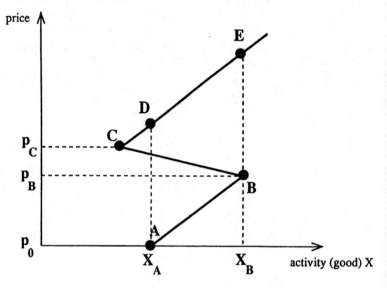

Figure 11.3   Negative slope of supply curve sets in when price is raised above p_B

3   Influences on the shape of the supply curve

The difference between the supply curve as suggested by traditional economic theory (shown in Figure 11.1) and the supply curve influenced by the Crowding-Out Effect (shown in Figures 11.2 and 11.3) depends on how far the conditions leading to an undermining of intrinsic motivation obtain. In Part I of this book, the following conditions relevant in this context have been identified.

The Crowding-Out Effect is larger

- the more personal the relationship between the person setting the price, and the person whose activity is to be influenced;
- the larger the extent of co-determination of the suppliers; and
- the more strongly the quantity supplied which is made contingent on the monetary reward in terms of the price paid.

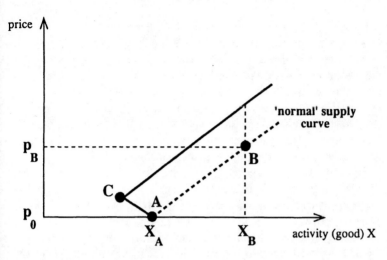

(a) Weak Crowding-Out Effect

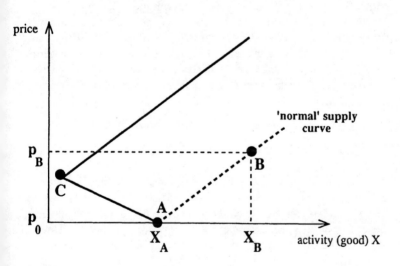

(b) Strong Crowding-Out Effect

*Figure 11.4   Relationship between 'normal' supply curve and supply
curve including crowding-out*

Figure 11.4a shows a constellation in which the Crowding-Out Effect is weak only, the two supply curves are close to each other. In the transactions considered 'typical' by traditional economics, a very large number of completely anonymous, impersonal actors trade with each other. An example is a computerized stock exchange where no crowding-out is induced at all, the two curves are identical and have a positive slope throughout. The same applies to many market activities in which the suppliers perform their services professionally, and without any relevant social interaction with the demanders paying the price.

Figure 11.4b shows the wide gap induced by a Crowding-Out Effect of large magnitude. In the extreme, namely, when the use of pricing destroys intrinsic motivation quickly and totally, and when the use of price incentives is unable to produce the supply at all, point C would be in the origin, and the supply curve would totally collapse. An example would be the relationship between close friends or lovers, where the inappropriate offer of a price for performing a service would suddenly destroy the intimacy and the intrinsic motivation along with it, and no amount of money can re-establish it. The supply curve pictured in Figure 11.4b is somewhat less spectacular. It may illustrate the supply response between acquaintances, one of whom offers the other a price for performing a service the other would have done for courtesy's sake (that is, intrinsically motivated). This leads to an angry reaction (movement from A to C). Once the friendship is destroyed (at C), the person can be induced to supply increasing amounts of the service when price is raised, but he or she does it now for purely extrinsic, egoistic reasons.

II   DOES CROWDING OUT MATTER AT ALL?

Sceptics might argue that all this fuss about crowding out intrinsic motivation is quite uninteresting and misleading. In order to increase the quantity of the good, or the extent of the activity to the level desired, it is only necessary to raise the price sufficiently. There is always a price at which this desired level can be achieved – exactly as predicted by traditional economic theory. The only exception is the extreme case in which the price system is not able to provide the supply at all, but this (as can be argued) is a largely irrelevant case. As the economists' saying goes: 'There is a price for everything'.

The only (minor) problem – it may further be argued – is to raise price sufficiently so that the quantity supplied does not fall in the ineffective intermediate range (between A and C in Figures 11.4 and 11.2, between B and C in Figure 11.3). But once this is done, the 'normal' supply curve takes over (in the range CDE), and all is well. The substitution of intrinsic motivation by monetary incentives need not be of any concern, it may even be welcome as it allows the policy-maker to fine-tune, that is, achieve the goals set with greater precision. There are three *counter arguments* against such sceptics.

1 Intrinsic motivation is a value in itself

Under important circumstances, it is not irrelevant what motives induce individuals to act. When creative, innovative, entrepreneurial, scientific and artistic services are desired, they are more efficiently supplied when the individuals concerned are intrinsically motivated (as shown in the last chapter). A substitution to monetary incentives is likely to decrease the quality of the service which is often not easily observable.

Another reason why the substitution of money-induced behaviour is undesirable or even rejected is the perceived value of the good produced. Many people, for instance, prefer to be cared for by their loving kin when they are ill and old (at least in so far as non-medical services go), and when it comes to dying, few prefer to end their days in the company of people who have been expressly paid for this service. This holds for European countries and even more so for the rest of the world, while it may be somewhat different in North America (but perhaps only because Americans normally no longer have the possibility to be cared for by their kin, and have therefore given up respective desires).

2 Cost Increase

When a Crowding-Out Effect takes place, the same quantity of supply is provided at a higher price (P_E instead of P_B in the preceding figures) than if no such effect existed. When the effect is strong, the price difference may be sizeable.

In the case of *individuals* demanding the good or activity, this may result in persons of low income no longer being able to consume the commodity because their budget prohibits it. The substitution of intrinsic by extrinsic motivation thus raises questions of income distribution and fairness. In each case it would have to be analysed how the distribution of opportunities looks like between the various income groups in society. While it is certainly not possible to provide a general answer, there is a nagging suspicion that the low income groups are often better off in a supply system based on intrinsic motivation than on monetary incentives.

To take the example of the previous subsection: it seems likely that the poor in Third World Countries are by far better off when old age care is undertaken in the family framework than if they had to buy the corresponding services on the market. One could well think that this result is in many cases obvious as an allocation over the price system is by definition more favourable to those who can invest the necessary money, that is, the high income recipients. But the issue is not quite so simple because one has to consider the additional possibilities of gaining monetary income when the price system is introduced. It might, for instance, be hypothesized that the low income recipients are especially competitive with regard to the market care for the sick and the old.

In the case of *governmental programmes* to raise the supply of a good or activity, more public funds are required when intrinsic motivation is crowded out. The necessary taxes can impose a substantial dead weight loss which raises the cost to society above the monetary revenue needed. Empirical studies suggest that the additional cost may be very high (see Stuart, 1984). The resistance to additional taxes leads to (legal) tax evasion and to (illegal) tax fraud which in turn are likely to undermine tax morale (Chapter 6). In any case, there will be political opposition to a rise in taxes so that it may be impossible to implement it at all. The required increase of the price (to p_E instead of p_B) in order to effect the same supply is in that case prevented by the governmental budget limit. To finance the rise in price by printing money also imposes cost in terms of various distortions (especially in terms of inflation); the same holds when the additional expenditure are financed by government debt.

3 Spill-Over Effect

A third reason why it does matter that there is a Crowding Effect relates to its negative consequences in areas beyond those where the price rise applies. The conditions under which intrinsic motivation is damaged in other areas as well have been identified (see Chapter 5). These conditions suggest that the Spill-Over Effect is in many cases relevant. A pertinent example has been presented for the case of environmental policy (see Chapter 7). When the area additionally affected by a fall in intrinsic motivation is amenable to monetary incentives, the damage may not be serious because the induced fall in supply can be compensated again by offering a higher price. If the price system is costly or impossible to apply, the induced loss in intrinsic motivation leads to a welfare loss which may make the initial use of pricing counterproductive.

The Spill-Over Effect makes it necessary for an effective economic policy to seriously consider the area beyond instrument application. This may be illustrated by the case of tax policy. Deterrence policy based on monitoring, and threat of punishment, is able to raise the tax revenue *ceteris paribus*, if the Crowding-Out Effect is weaker than the Price Effect. But there are two major undesired side effects to be reckoned with:

(a) A *reduction in tax morale* may be induced which affects the whole tax system. The incentives to reduce the tax burden are fostered and a multitude of means to evade taxes are newly created, and actively exploited by the tax subjects. Tax consultants are hired to fight against the government (an option which is beyond consideration in a society with high tax morale); activities are chosen which allow higher deductibles; occupations are selected which (for one reason or another) are less taxed; more (untaxed) leisure is taken; one moves one's assets out of the country or finally leaves it physically. Reduced tax morale also induces citizens to cheat more on taxes: it is well known that an almost indefinite number of opportunities for such behaviour exists.

Experience, as well as empirical research (see for example, Slemrod, 1992), shows that precious little can be done to check tax evasion and fraud. Each measure to fight it tends to reduce tax morale further (as long as it is not strictly, and efficiently, directed against tax cheaters only) and fosters individuals' imagination to relieve their tax burden. As discussed (in Chapter 6), the tax revenue observed cannot be explained by deterrence, that is, by applying the traditional model of maximizing subjective (egoistic) utility subject to expected punishment. For that reason, a fall in tax morale induced by the higher public revenue requirements has to be taken seriously and cannot be dismissed out of hand.

(b) The need to raise government revenue may, beyond taxation, more generally crowd out the sense of *civic virtue*. As a consequence, a negative attitude towards the state becomes current currency, which destroys the basis for a functioning democracy. There are also direct economic consequences. Rent-seeking activity becomes more prominent, which means that an increasing share of effort is put into socially unproductive endeavours, in particular to get benefits out of the government. There will be increased lobbying to introduce new tax exemptions and deductibles, to get public subsidies and pensions of all sorts, and – more difficult to detect – protection against competition. All these rent-seeking activities lead to additional distortions reducing a society's production capacities, that is, they constitute real cost for society.

All this shows that the (so-called) side effects of raising government revenue to pay for the increased supply price (p_E instead of p_B) may have serious consequences; in any case they may not be considered lightly even though some of the effects are indirect and (presumably) take place only after some time. The three counter arguments discussed in this section – (1) intrinsic motivation is desired, (2) cost increase, and (3) Spill-Over Effect – are of major importance. It *does* matter when Crowding Effects occur.

III   WHAT TO DO?

Before policy advisers suggest a particular policy, and before politicians engage on it, they should check carefully whether Crowding Effects (and Spill-Over Effects) are likely to occur, and if so, what size they are likely to be.

Under many circumstances, Crowding Effects will not occur as the conditions identified in this text are not met. This applies, as has repeatedly been said, to those areas where anonymous traders interact with each other. But these areas do not correspond to the markets on which traditional economic theory concentrates. Most importantly, the labour market is not generally characterized by abstract trades. Rather, personal interactions, as well as ideas of co-determination, play a large role, making the labour market amenable to Crowding Effects (as shown in the last chapter).

An effective policy requires that the conditions for the appearance of Crowding Effects are carefully evaluated. If they are taken to be immanent, there are two options:

(i)   Instruments which from the point of view of the Price Effect are less efficient, must be taken into consideration if they support, or at least do not damage, *intrinsic motivation*. An example is environmental subsidies which appear to be less efficient than tradeable licences, but which carry the notion that it is good at protecting the environment and strengthening environmental morale.

(ii) To forsake government intervention. Even if a policy instrument looks efficient from the purely 'technical' point of view, its overall effects may be counterproductive if the cumulated negative consequences of having undermined intrinsic motivation are taken into account. In that case, *no policy is the best policy*.

This second option mirrors the case against activism in macro-economic policy based on the cost of wrong timing, but even more prominently on the Rational Expectations Revolution suggesting policy ineffectiveness (under specified conditions; see, for example, Minford, 1992; Attfield, Demery and Duck, 1991). However, these reasons are completely different from the Crowding Effect here discussed, and therefore quite different policy responses are in order:

(a) When crowding-out obtains, an effort should be made to maintain and promote intrinsic motivation. This also refers to the constitutional level and suggests laws acknowledging citizens' rights and civic virtue (see Chapter 6). The Rational Expectations Revolution merely suggests that a stable institutional environment be provided, and that fine-tuning interventions by government be prevented.

The need to foster intrinsic motivation, be it in the form of civic virtue, tax, work or environmental morale, imposes a completely new task to economists for which they are ill prepared because they have so far tended to neglect these sources of motivation. It will certainly be necessary to look at the neighbouring social sciences of sociology, psychology and political science on how to deal with these notions, and what policies they suggest for fostering intrinsic motivation. However, simply referring to social upbringing and education is not sufficient, because they are imprecise and indicate only broadly in which direction to go. Moreover, they are partial, as it is well possible that intrinsic motivation can be raised more directly. In any case, economists have to learn a lot in order to be able to provide useful policy advice.

One means of raising intrinsic motivation in the form of regard for others is discussion. When individuals are able to talk to each other, they exhibit more solidarity and behave more cooperatively. This effect is strongly supported by experimental evidence (see, for example, the survey by Sally, 1995). Thus, experiments undertaken by us at the University of Zurich in 1993/4 (Bohnet and Frey, 1994; Frey and Bohnet, 1995, 1996) reveal that under anony-

mous conditions only 12 per cent of the participants were prepared to act cooperatively in a four-person Prisoner's Dilemma
Game. When they were allowed to talk to each other before the
game, and to establish an atmosphere of higher confidence, 78 per
cent of them behaved in a cooperative way. They were thus intrinsically motivated to contribute to the establishment of a public
good, though the decision itself was taken privately. Similarly, in
a Dictator Game,[2] the allocator shares the sum received equally
with the recipient if they are previously able to establish verbal
communication, while under anonymous conditions the allocator
passes on only 26 per cent. These experimental results suggest
that intrinsic values such as other-regarding or solidaric behaviour
can be fostered by the interaction among people. There are certainly limits to that possibility; in some cases closer interaction
produces hostility and less cooperation.

(b)   The second policy response which differs fundamentally from much
current theory of economic policy is to put faith in individuals'
intrinsic motivation. Exactly when a substantial Crowding Effect is
to be expected, human behaviour is strongly determined by intrinsic motivation. Such faith is related to ideas coveted by quite different strands of social science (only very partly economics). Despite
its deadly distortion by communism, humanistic socialism holds
that individuals are intrinsically motivated if only they live under
suitable conditions. The approach here championed is miles away
from the ideology that the 'good' human beings are prevented by
capitalism and the market. Rather, it has been emphasized that
regulations which are rampant in real socialism also tend to crowd
out intrinsic motivation, and in many cases do so more strongly and
more quickly (Chapter 4). Similar views as in anti-market socialism
are held in the cooperative and co-determinist movements which
hold that workers are more motivated when they are not bound by
capitalist labour contracts. As the discussion of compensation
schemes (see Chapter 10) has shown, the possibility of co-deter-
mining is at best one factor raising work morale. Co-determination
is, moreover, only relevant for work motivation in so far as it relates
to an individual's work place, but it is of little consequence when it
comes to more general concepts of co-determination, say, on investment projects. The recent appeal to communitarianism (see, for
example, Etzioni, 1988; Bell, 1993) is also much broader and is
therefore only indirectly related to the ideas here discussed. It would

have to be established in a precise way how communitarian forms of living support intrinsic motivation. So far, this relationship has only been postulated but not established. The analysis pursued here starts from a quite different angle, namely experimental social psychology. This approach should not only help us to see the importance and consequences of the Crowding Effect, but also to find means to maintain and foster intrinsic motivation where it is desired.

NOTES

1. In the meantime, Becker has started to deal with traditions, norms and values in a fascinating way, see Becker (1992).
2. One person, the allocator, is given a sum of money and is free to give all or nothing, or any amount in between, to a second person, the recipient. Formal game theory based on egoism predicts that the allocator does not pass anything to the recipient irrespective of whether the players previously talked to each other or not (so-called 'cheap talk'; see Kahneman, Knetsch and Thaler, 1986a and b; Johnson, 1993). An analogous result holds for a similar game, the Ultimatum Game; see Güth, Schmittberger and Schwarze, 1982; Güth and Tietz, 1990.

SUGGESTED FURTHER READINGS

The basic premises of the economic model of human behaviour and its most recent developments are presented in

Becker, Gary S. (1996), *Accounting for Tastes*, Cambridge: Harvard University Press.

Co-determination is discussed in

Overbeck, Egon (1984), 'Co-Determination at Company Level', in Wolfram Engels and Hans Pohl (eds), *German Yearbook on Business History 1983*, New York; Berlin and Tokyo: Springer, pp. 11–17.

A special view of human beings is presented by communitarians of which one of the most important is

Etzioni, Amitai (1988), *The Moral Dimension. Towards a New Economics*, New York: Free Press.

The importance of intrinsic motivation in the form of trust and civic virtues is highlighted in

Fukuyama, Francis (1995), *Trust: The Social Virtues and the Creation of Prosperity*, New York: Free Press.

A more economically oriented analysis is provided, for example, in

Ghoshal, Sumantra and Peter Moran (1995), 'Bad for Practice: A Critique of Transaction Cost Theory', in Dorothy P. Moore (ed.), *Academy of Management, Best Papers Proceedings*, Madison: Omnipress, pp. 12–16.

12. Consequences for economic theory

Consideration of the Crowding Effect leads to a richer (section I) and more psychological (section II) model of human behaviour. The corresponding model of man is called '*Homo Oeconomicus Maturus*' (*HOM*) to distinguish it from the concept commonly used in economics, but also from other extensions of *Homo Oeconomicus*. Section III discusses whether these refinements should be integrated in an *overarching* model of human behaviour.

I   A RICHER MODEL OF MAN

The concept of man currently used in economics (see Becker, 1976, 1993; Kirchgässner, 1991) assumes that individuals maximize their own utility subjects to the constraints imposed most importantly by income and time. He or she is taken to be egoistic and to be interested mainly – and sometimes wholly – in material values only (wealth maximization hypothesis). This is the crude model of *Homo Oeconomicus* which has proved able to explain a surprisingly large share of human behaviour. It has been subjected to many empirical tests, and has performed well also compared to competing models of human behaviour (Hirshleifer, 1985; Frey, 1992a).

For some purposes, especially for applications outside the strictly economic (market) sphere, various scholars have suggested extending the *Homo Oeconomicus*. Thus, Becker (1981) has introduced altruism to account for behaviour in the familial context, in particular the relationship of parents to their offspring. Akerlof (1984) has integrated prestige and social norms to explain social exchange more fully.

This book has presented a particular extension of the economic model of man. The corresponding human being is called '*Homo Oeconomicus Maturus*' (*HOM*). This man is more 'mature' in the sense that he is endowed with a more refined motivational structure, leading to the four basic propositions heralded in the Preface: (1) Intrinsic motivation presents an important determinant of human behaviour; (2) Monetary incentives (under identifiable conditions) undermine intrinsic motivation (Crowding-Out Effect); (3) Other interventions external to a particular individual may also produce a Crowding-Out Effect, that is, in addition to monetary (material) incentives this applies also to regulations with their commands, controls and punishments; and (4) Under some (rather rare) conditions external interventions bolster intrinsic motivation (Crowding-In Effect).

HOM stands in clear contrast to the classical *Homo Oeconomicus*. The latter's most central, and universally valid, prediction is the Price Effect (Becker, 1976; Stigler, 1984) stating that a higher monetary reward (price) induces more of an activity. For supply, this principle produces a positive relationship between price and quantity; for demand where the respective price is a cost, it produces a negative relationship between price and quantity. The Price Effect is easily generalized. 'Price' may take on many meanings, it not only denotes 'rewards' in the case of supply and 'cost' in the case of demand, but extends to non-material units such as, for instance, to cost in terms of loss of prestige.

HOM is also in definite contrast to other extensions of *Homo Oeconomicus*. They accept the Price Effect but interpret it in a more differentiated way (see below).

HOM also accepts the Price Effect as a basic behavioural principle but adds the Crowding Effect so that the positive relationship posited for supply, and the negative one for demand, is no longer generally valid. *Homo Oeconomicus Maturus* allows for a 'Perverse Relationship' where a monetary payment (price) results in a reduction of the corresponding activity. The Price Effect is not affected but amended in an empirically important direction. As a result, a richer model of human behaviour is constructed wherein the Crowding Effect dominates the Price Effect under some conditions.

Homo Oeconomicus Maturus allows a 'behavioural anomaly' in the sense of a systematic deviation from traditional *Homo Oeconomicus* (for surveys see, for example, Dawes, 1988; Frey and Eichenberger, 1989; Thaler, 1987, 1992). A great number of such anomalies have over the last years been identified:

- The Reference Point Effect. People evaluate alternatives not in terms of total wealth but relative to a reference point of which the prevailing condition is most prominent. It is in this case called the Status Quo Effect.

- Sunk Cost Effect. People tend to take forgone cost into account in their decisions even though they refer to the past and do not influence future options.
- Endowment Effect. A good in a person's endowment is valued more highly than those not held in the endowment.
- Framing Effects. The way a decision problem is formulated, and the way the information is presented, have a marked effect on individual decisions.
- Availability Bias. Recent, spectacular and personally experienced events are overestimated when people take a decision.
- Representativeness Bias. People systematically misconceive prior probabilities, and are insensitive to sample size.
- Opportunity Cost Effect. Out-of-pocket monetary cost is given greater weight in the decision calculus than opportunity cost of the same size.
- Certainty Effect. Outcomes obtained with certainty are attributed greater weight in people's decisions than those which are uncertain even when the known expected utilities are the same.

All these anomalies are inconsistent with the model of man used in modern economic theory. In particular, they systematically violate the von Neumann–Morgenstern axioms of rationality, which means that the commonly used subjective expected utility maximization model is no longer appropriate (Schoemaker, 1982; Machina, 1987). However, it turns out that while disturbing, none of these anomalies consistently violates the Price Effect. They certainly mitigate or weaken it, but they do *not* reverse it. Even in the presence of these anomalies, one can rely on a price rise inducing an increase in supply, and a decrease in demand, especially at the aggregate level (see Frey and Eichenberger, 1994). In contrast, *Homo Oeconomicus Maturus* (*HOM*) under identifiable conditions reacts in the opposite direction – supply is reduced, and an activity is undertaken less intensively. *HOM* thus constitutes a more radical departure from existing models of man without rejecting the Price Effect. What *HOM* does is to determine under which conditions, or in which area, the Price Effect guides human behaviour, and under which conditions Crowding Effects are to be expected.

II A MORE PSYCHOLOGICAL MAN

Homo Oeconomicus Maturus takes a psychological effect – the 'hidden cost of reward' – which is important in economic affairs, generalizes it and integrates it into economic theory. The resulting Crowding Effect is well compatible with economic reasoning. It can be modelled as a substitution effect where individuals reduce the motivation under their control (intrinsic motivation) when an external intervention by pricing or regulating confronts them with an extrinsic motivation.

There have been several previous efforts to introduce specific psychological effects into economic theory. Most prominent examples are

- Scitovsky (1976, 1981) builds on Wundt's Law of the optimal degree of arousal, and refers to it as the 'desire for excitement'.
- Leibenstein (1976) develops the notion of an 'inert area', from where individuals have no incentive to depart even when utility increasing opportunities arise. A related idea has been coined 'ipsative behaviour' (Frey and Foppa, 1986; Frey, 1992a, ch. 12). It adds to the objective and the subjective (personally perceived) opportunity set of behaviour a third, radically different one: the 'ipsative' opportunity set refers to *oneself* only, and determines one's own behaviour. What matters, for instance, is not what the objective probability of getting cancer is, nor what one thinks it is (subjective probability), but how likely one believes that one gets cancer oneself. That the ipsative opportunity set may drastically differ from the objective and subjective one, and may do so for extended periods, can be seen when it comes to divorce. Everyone knows of the high risk of marriage splitting up, but the vast majority of people believe that this happens to others, not to themselves. The systematic ipsative over- or underestimation of one's possibility set has been empirically supported for a wide number of behaviours (see Weinstein, 1980).
- Hirschman (1958, 1970) inquires into the conditions under which artistic activity, entrepreneurship and innovation can be awakened. He thus does not take the effort expended as given. One possibility of activating people is to consciously create imbalances, because it induces and even forces people to become active in order to survive, or at least to maintain their level of living.
- Simon (1957, 1982), Selten and Tietz (1980) and Williamson (1985) propagate that individuals are incapable of maximizing in

any strict sense and propose the concept of 'bounded rationality' as a more realistic, and psychologically adequate alternative which takes into account cognitive limitations of human thinking.

- Schelling (1978, 1980), Thaler and Shefrin (1981) and several other scholars (for example, Sen, 1977) develop the concept of 'self-commitment'. Persons who are aware that under particular conditions they fall prey to a temptation, can try to evade the trap by binding themselves. An example is Ulysses, who had himself fastened to the mast of his ship in order not to succumb to the sirens' chant. Such theoretical ideas establish a relationship to psychological theories of how to master one's life.
- Schlicht (1979) employs Gestalt theory to explain the movement toward labour management.
- Akerlof and Dickens (1982), Gilad, Kaish and Loeb (1987) and various other economists use the psychological notion of 'cognitive dissonance' (Festinger, 1957) to account for beliefs and consequent behaviour which otherwise is difficult to explain in the economic framework. They show in particular, that rational workers discount the risk they are exposed to in their job, and that they therefore use less safety equipment than in a less risky occupation.
- Frank (1988) attributes emotions which are trustworthy as they are difficult to give signals (such as blushing) a role in economic models of human behaviour. This aspect is firmly based in psychological thinking.
- In surveys (Kahneman, Knetsch and Thaler, 1986a; Frey and Pommerehne, 1993) and experiments (for example, Güth, Schmittberger and Schwarze, 1982; Kahneman, Knetsch and Thaler, 1986b; also Bohnet and Frey, 1995; Frey and Bohnet, 1995), the notion of 'fairness' as applied to economic issues has been explored for a large number of conditions (a review is provided, for example, by Roth, 1995). Fairness in terms of 'reciprocity' (see the experiments by Fehr, Kirchsteiger and Riedl, 1993; and the survey by Camerer and Thaler, 1995) draw directly on the notions of equity developed in psychology (Gouldner, 1960; Adams, 1965; Walster, Walster and Berscheid, 1977).

Some of these efforts to integrate psychological effects into economics have been noted by mainstream economists in the sense that they are (often almost ritually) quoted at the appropriate moments, but they have had precious little effect on economic theory as a whole. The classical *Homo Oeconomicus* is still used as a matter of course. The reason presumably is that these extended versions are not sufficiently different from the simple model of wealth maximization. The special features highlighted in the psychological effects are felt to be irrelevant under most circumstances. This position may well be tenable in some old-established fields of economics in which abstract markets dominate but it is most doubtful as soon as one goes beyond.

Some authors have pursued a second strategy, namely, to break completely with neo-classical economics and its *Homo Oeconomicus*, and to construct a 'psychological economics' in which the human beings acting correspond to the ideas and requirements of psychology (see, for instance, Furnham and Lewis, 1986; Lea, Tarpy and Webly, 1987). While such attempts are courageous, they are completely disregarded within economics for several reasons. Modern economics as the self-proclaimed 'queen of the social sciences' has achieved a well-defined core of assumptions and models which are protected against criticism. Competition among economists for publication and academic position is increasingly intensive and moves to an international level. Especially, young economists only have a chance to be successful if they stay within the defined limits and make themselves known by incremental, but easily publishable variations of accepted models (see Frey and Eichenberger, 1993, 1997). Another explanation for the rejection of a completely new, psychological model of man is that (at least so far) few empirically testable propositions relevant for economics have been derived. In view of this shortcoming, it is relatively easy to reject these efforts as irrelevant, or simply to disregard them.

The attempt discussed in this book seeks to circumvent this problem by introducing a well-defined and particular psychological effect into the existing framework of economic theory. Introducing *one* psychological effect at one time accentuates the difference from existing theory. Testable propositions can be derived, and corresponding empirical analyses can be undertaken.

III   TOWARDS AN OVERARCHING MODEL OF HUMAN BEHAVIOUR?

Is it not a desirable goal to have a model of man integrating the different psychological effects found to be important for economics? It would certainly be good to have such a model but this goal is difficult, if not impossible to achieve.[1]

To integrate one particular effect, on the other hand, is more manageable than trying to construct a more comprehensive model. There always lurks the danger of just superimposing or juxtaposing psychological features to *Homo Oeconomicus*. It sounds, of course, attractive to combine 'economic', 'sociological', psychological', 'political', 'cultural' and 'biological' man, but in practice this normally amounts to a play of words. The attempt fails as long as the relative importance of each type is unknown, the conditions under which one type or the other dominates are unspecified, and the interaction between the various types is left open.

There is also a disadvantage connected with an overarching model. By necessity, it will have to be extremely complex, and one of the major advantages of *Homo Oeconomicus* is given up. Moreover, the individual psychological effects must be stripped to the bare bones in order to be able to integrate them in one model; the result may well be that the 'spirit' of the various psychological effects gets lost and that a rather mechanistic model remains.

There is a practical, and possibly more desirable, alternative to building an overarching model of man. It leaves the partial models including some specific psychological effects as they are, and relegates the task of choosing the 'appropriate' model to the problem at hand. This pragmatic approach leaves the question open, what type of human behaviour is appropriate for what task. This also constitutes a chance for economic science. It forces the researchers first to consider seriously what the social problem to be analysed really is, and only to then embark on manipulating a particular model. This procedure stands in contrast to much of what is done in modern economics, where the model often stands at the beginning, and one looks thereafter where it could be applied. Often enough the applications are rather trivial and concentrate on the 'strong links' while the 'weak links' are left aside (see Mayer, 1993). To reverse the procedure by putting the problem first, and the choice among various models of human behaviour second, could turn economics from a technique driven science into an art. The skilful choice among the various types of *Homines Oeconomici* would differentiate masters from simple technicians. The use of an appropriate model of human behaviour – an important version of which is Crowding Theory – to analyse a particular social problem requires judgement, experience and involvement: knowledge of a deeper kind would bc valucd again.

NOTE

1. The even simpler exercise of integrating the psychological anomalies mentioned above within a single model has so far proved to be unsuccessful. Various generalizations of the expected utility maximization model, as well as models going beyond expected utility maximization have only been able to account for some, but not all anomalies. In particular, framing effects could so far not be integrated (see Machina, 1987), nor are they likely to be in the future (Frey and Eichenberger, 1994).

SUGGESTED FURTHER READINGS

A general analysis of methodological issues is presented in
Blaug, Mark (1992), *The Methodology of Economics, Or How Economists Explain* (2nd edn), Cambridge: Cambridge University Press.
Mayer, Thomas (1993), *Truth versus Precision in Economics*, Aldershot: Edward Elgar.
An opening up of the narrow model of human behaviour has been suggested by
Becker, Gary S. (1992), 'Habits, Addictions and Traditions', *Kyklos*, **45**, 327–46.
Denzau, Arthur T. and Douglass C. North (1994), 'Shared Mental Models, Ideologies and Institutions', *Kyklos*, **47**, 3–31.
Behavioural anomalies are treated in
Thaler, Robert H. (1992), *The Winner's Curse. Paradoxes and Anomalies in Economic Life*, New York: Free Press.
Frey, Bruno S. and Reiner Eichenberger (1994), 'Economic Incentives Transform Psychological Anomalies', *Journal of Economic Behavior and Organization*, **23**, 215–34.
Particularly noteworthy psychological extensions of *Homo Oeconomicus* are
Scitovsky, Tibor (1976), *The Joyless Economy: An Inquiry into Human Satisfaction and Dissatisfaction*, Oxford: Oxford University Press.
Hirschman, Albert O. (1970), *Exit, Voice and Loyalty*, Cambridge, MA.: Harvard University Press.
Akerlof, George A. 1984), *An Economic Theorist's Book of Tales*, Cambridge: Cambridge University Press.
Frank, Robert H. (1988), *Passions Within Reason. The Strategic Role of Emotions*, New York: Norton.

References

Adams, J. Stacey (1963), 'Towards an Understanding of Inequity', *Journal of Abnormal and Social Psychology*, **67** (November), 422–36.

Adams, J. Stacey (1965), 'Injustice in Social Exchange', in Leonard Berkowitz (ed.), *Advances in Experimental Social Psychology*, **2**, New York: Academic Press, 267–99.

Akerlof, George A. (1984), *An Economic Theorist's Book of Tales*, Cambridge: Cambridge University Press.

Akerlof, George A. (1989), 'The Economics of Illusion', *Economics and Politics*, **1** (Spring), 1–15.

Akerlof, George A. and William T. Dickens (1982), 'The Economic Consequences of Cognitive Dissonance', *American Economic Review*, **72** (June), 307–19.

Akerlof, George A. and Janet L. Yellen (1986), *Efficiency Wage Models and the Labor Market*, Cambridge: Cambridge University Press.

Alchian, Armen A. (1977), *Economic Forces at Work*, Indianapolis: Liberty Press.

Alchian, Armen A. and Harold Demsetz (1972), 'Production, Information Costs and Economic Organization', *American Economic Review*, **62** (December), 777–95.

Allingham, Michael G. and Agnar Sandmo (1972), 'Income Tax Evasion: A Theoretical Analysis', *Journal of Public Economics*, **1** (November), 323–38.

Alm, James, Betty Jackson and Michael McKee (1992), 'Deterrence and Beyond: Toward a Kinder, Gentler IRS', in Joel Slemrod (ed.), *Why People Pay Taxes*, Ann Arbor: University of Michigan Press, 311–29.

Alm, James, Isabel Sanchez and Ana de Juan (1995), 'Economic and Noneconomic Factors in Tax Compliance', *Kyklos*, **48** (1), 3–18.

Anderson, Martin (ed.) (1976), *Conscription. A Select and Annotated Bibliography*, Stanford: Hoover Institution Press.

Anderson, Martin (ed.) (1982), *The Military Draft. Selected Readings on Conscription*, Stanford: Hoover Institution Press.

Andrews, I.R. (1967), 'Wage Inequity and Job Performance: An Experimental Study', *Journal of Applied Psychology*, **51**, 39–45.

Aoki, Masahiko (1990), 'Towards an Economic Model of the Japanese Firm', *Journal of Economic Literature*, **28** (March), 1–27.

Argyris, Chris and Donald A. Schön (1978), *Organizational Learning: A Theory of Action Perspective*, Reading, MA: Davidson.

Arnold, H.J. (1976), 'Effects of Performance Feedback and Extrinsic Reward upon High Intrinsic Motivation', *Organizational Behavior and Human Performance*, **17**, 275–88.

Aronfreed, J. (1968), *Conduct and Conscience*, New York: Academic Press.

Arrow, Kenneth J. (1970), 'Political and Economic Evaluation of Social Effects and Externalities', in Julius Margolis (ed.), *The Analysis of Public Output*, New York: Columbia University Press, 1–23.

Arrow, Kenneth J. (1972), 'Gifts and Exchanges', *Philosophy and Public Affairs*, **1**, 343–62.

Arrow, Kenneth J. (1975), 'Gifts and Exchanges', in Edmund Phelps (ed.), *Altruism, Morality and Economic Theory*, New York: Sage, 13–28.

Attfield, C.L.F, D. Demery and N.W. Duck (1991), *Rational Expectations in Macroeconomics: An Introduction to Theory and Evidence* (2nd edn), Oxford and Cambridge: Blackwell.

Attfield, R. (1993), *The Ethics of Environmental Concern*, New York: Columbia University Press.

Baker, George P., Michael C. Jensen and Kevin J. Murphy (1988), 'Compensation and Incentives: Practice versus Theory', *Journal of Finance*, **43** (July), 593–616.

Bardach, Eugene and Robert A. Kagan (1982), *Going By the Book: The Problem of Regulatory Unreasonableness*, Philadelphia: Temple University Press.

Barkema, Harry G. (1995), 'Do Job Executives Work Harder When they are Monitored?', *Kyklos*, **48**, 19–42.

Baumol, William J. and Wallace E. Oates (1979), *Economics, Environmental Policy, and the Quality of Life*, Englewood Cliffs, NJ: Prentice-Hall.

Becker, Gary S. (1968), 'Crime and Punishment: An Economic Approach', *Journal of Political Economy*, **76**, 169–217.

Becker, Gary S. (1976), *The Economic Approach to Human Behavior*, Chicago: Chicago University Press.

Becker, Gary S. (1981), *A Treatise on the Family*, Cambridge, MA: Harvard University Press.

Becker, Gary S. (1992),'Habits, Addictions, and Traditions', *Kyklos*, **45** (3), 327–46.

Becker, Gary S. (1993), 'Nobel Lecture: The Economic Way of Looking at Behavior', *Journal of Political Economy*, **101**, 385–409.

Becker, Gary S. and George J. Stigler (1975), 'Law Enforcement, Malfeasance, and Compensation of Enforcers', *Journal of Legal Studies*, **65**, 314–25.

Beer, Michael, Bert Spector, Paul R. Lawrence, D. Quinn Mills and Richard E. Walton (1984), *Managing Human Assets*, New York: Macmillan.

Bell, Daniel (1976), *The Cultural Contradictions of Capitalism*, New York: Basic Books.

Bell, Daniel (1993), *Communitarianism and its Critics*, Oxford: Clarendon Press.

Billings, Elden E. (1971), 'The Civil War and Conscription', *Current History*, **55** (June), 333–66.

Blinder, Alan S. (1987), *Hard Heads, Soft Hearts*, Reading, MA: Addison-Wesley.

Bohnet, Iris and Bruno S. Frey (1994), 'Direct-democratic Rules: The Role of Discussion', *Kyklos*, **47**, 341–54.

Bohnet, Iris and Bruno S. Frey (1995), 'Ist Reden Silber und Schweigen Gold? Eine ökonomische Analyse', *Zeitschrift für Wirtschafts- und Sozialwissenschaften*, **115**, 169–209.

Bonacich, P. (1986), 'Contributions to Churches: A Research Proposal', in Henk A. Wilke, Dave M. Messick and Christel G. Rutte (eds), *Experimental Social Dilemmas*, Frankfurt (Main): Lang, 77–86.

Brennan, Geoffrey and James M. Buchanan (1983), 'Predictive Power and the Choice among Regimes', *Economic Journal*, **93** (March), 89–105.

Brennan, Geoffrey and James M. Buchanan (1985), *The Reason of Rules. Constitutional Political Economy*, Cambridge: Cambridge University Press.

Brennan, Geoffrey and Hamlin, A. (1995), 'Economizing on Virtue', *Constitutional Political Economy*, **6**, 35–6.

Browning, Edgar K. (1987), 'On the Marginal Welfare Cost of Taxation', *American Economic Review*, **77** (1), 11–23.

Buchanan, James M. (1985), 'The Moral Dimension of Debt Financing', *Economic Inquiry*, **23** (January), 1–5.

Buchanan, James M. (1987), 'Constitutional Economics', in John Eatwell, Milgate Murray and Peter Newman (eds), *The New Palgrave: A Dictionary of Economics*, London: Macmillan, 585–8.

Buchanan, James M. (1994), 'Choosing What to Choose', *Journal of Institutional and Theoretical Economics* (JITE), **150** (1), 123–35.

Camerer, Colin and Richard H. Thaler (1995), 'Anomalies: Ultimatums, Dictators and Manners', *Journal of Economic Perspectives*, **9** (Spring), 209–19.

Cameron, Judy and W. David Pierce (1994), 'Reinforcement, Reward, and Intrinsic Motivation: A Meta-Analysis', *Review of Educational Research*, **64** (Fall), 363–423.

Carnes, S.A. *et al.* (1983), 'Incentives and Nuclear Waste Siting', *Energy Systems and Policy*, **7** (4), 324–51.

Cialdini, Robert B. (1989), 'Social Motivations to Comply: Norms, Values and Principles', in Jeffrey A. Roth and John T. Scholz (eds), *Taxpayer Compliance*, vol. 2, Philadelphia: University of Pennsylvania Press, 200–227.

Coase, Ronald H. (1978), 'Economics and Contiguous Disciplines', *Journal of Law, Economics and Organization*, **4** (Spring), 33–47.

Coleman, James S. (1990), *Foundations of Social Theory*, Cambridge, MA: Harvard University Press.

Collard, David (1978), '*Altruism and the Economy: A Study of Non-Selfish Economics*, London: Martin Robertson.

Condorcet, Marquis de (1795), *Esquisse d'un tableau historique du progrès de l'esprit humain*, Paris: Diannyaere.

Condry, John and James Chambers (1978), 'Intrinsic Motivation and the Process of Learning' in Mark R. Lepper and David Greene (eds), *The Hidden Costs of Rewards: New Perspectives on the Psychology of Human Motivation*, Hillsdale, NJ: Erlbaum, 61–83.

Congleton, Roger D. (1991), 'The Economic Role of a Work Ethic', *Journal of Economic Behavior and Organization*, **15**, 365–85.

Cooper, Michael H. and Anthony J. Culyer (1973), 'The Economics of Giving and Selling Blood' in *The Economics of Charity*, London: Institute of Economic Affairs, 109–43.

Cooter, Robert D. (1984), Prices and Sanctions, *Columbia Law Review*, **84**, 1523–60.

Cooter, Robert D. (1994), 'Laws and Prices: How Economics Contributed to Law by Misunderstanding Morality', Working Paper No. 94–2, Program in Law and Economics, University of California at Berkeley.

Cowell, Frank A. (1990), *Cheating the Government. The Economics of Evasion*, Cambridge, MA: MIT Press.

Crandall, Robert W. and John D. Graham (1984), 'Automobile Safety Regulation and Offsetting Behavior: Some New Empirical Estimates', *American Economic Review*, **74** (2) (May), 328–31.

Cropper, Maureen L. and Wallace E. Oates (1992), 'Environmental Economics: A Survey', *Journal of Economic Literature*, **30** (June), 675–740.

Curtis, Craig, Quint C. Turman and David C. Nice (1991), 'Improving Legal Compliance by Noncoercive Means. Coproducing Order in Washington State', *Social Science Quarterly*, **72**, 645–60.

Darity, William and Arthur H. Goldsmith (1996), 'Social Psychology, Unemployment and Macroeconomics', *Journal of Economic Perspectives*, **10** (Winter), 121–40.

Dawes, Robyn M. (1988), *Rational Choice in an Uncertain World*, San Diego and New York: Harcourt, Brace, Yovanovich.

De Alessi, Louis (1983), 'Property Rights, Transaction Costs and X-Efficiency: An Essay in Economic Theory', *American Economic Review*, **73** (March), 64–81.

DeCharms, R. (1968), *Personal Causation: The Internal Affective Determinants of Behavior*, New York: Academic Press.

Deci, Edward L. (1971), 'Effects of Externally Mediated Rewards on Intrinsic Motivation', *Journal of Personality and Social Psychology*, **18**, 105–15.

Deci, Edward L. (1972), 'Intrinsic Motivation, Extrinsic Reinforcement and Inequity', *Journal of Personality and Social Psychology*, **22**, 113–20.

Deci, Edward L. (1975), *Intrinsic Motivation*, New York: Plenum Press.

Deci, Edward L. (1978), Applications of Research on the Effects of Rewards' in Mark R. Lepper and David Greene (eds), *The Hidden Costs of Reward*, Hillsdale, NY: Erlbaum, 193–203.

Deci, Edward, L. (1987), 'The Support of Autonomy and the Control of Behavior, *Journal of Personality and Social Psychology*, **53**, 1024–37.

Deci, Edward L. and Richard M. Ryan (1980), 'The Empirical Exploration of Intrinsic Motivational Processes', *Advances in Experimental Social Psychology*, **10**, 39–80.

Deci, Edward L. and Richard M. Ryan (1985), *Intrinsic Motivation and Self-Determination in Human Behavior*, New York: Plenum Press.

Des Jardins, Joseph R. (1993), *Environmental Ethics*, Belmont, CA: Wadsworth.

Diamond, Peter A. and Jerry A. Hausman (1994), 'Contingent Valuation: Is Some Number Better than No Number?', *Journal of Economic Perpectives*, **8** (4), Fall, 45–64.

Dickens, William T. (1986), 'Crime and Punishment Again: the Economic Approach with a Psychological Twist', *Journal of Public Economics*, **30**, 109–16.

Dixon, John and Robert P. Scheurell (1989), 'Social Welfare in Developed Market Countries: Preface', in John D. Dixon and Robert P. Scheurell, *Social Welfare in Developed Market Countries. Comparative Social Welfare Series*, London and New York: Routledge, vii–xii.

Donaldson, Les (1980), *Behavior Supervision*, Reading, MA: Addison-Wesley.

Downey, Gary L. (1985), 'Federalism and Nuclear Waste Disposal: The Struggle Over Shared Decision Making, *Journal of Policy Analysis and Management*, **5**(1), 73–99.

Drake, Alvin; S.N. Finkelstein and H.M. Sapolsky (1982), *The American Blood Supply*, Cambridge, MA: MIT Press.

Dryzek, John S. (1992), *Discursive Democracy. Politics, Policy and Political Science*, Cambridge: Cambridge University Press.

Durkheim, Emile (1964) [1893], *The Division of Labor in Society*, New York: Free Press.

Easterling, Douglas and Howard Kunreuther (1995), *The Dilemma of Siting a High-Level Nuclear Waste Repository*, Boston: Kluwer.

Easton, David (1975), 'A Reassessment of the Concept of Political Support', *British Journal of Political Science*, **5**, 435–57.

Eckert, Ross D. (1985), 'Blood, Money and Monopoly', in Ross D. Eckert (ed.), *Securing a Safer Blood Supply: Two Views*, Washington and London: American Enterprise Institute for Public Policy Research.

Elster, Jon (1989), 'Social Norms and Economic Theory', *Journal of Economic Perspectives*, **3** (Fall), 99–119.

Etzioni, Amitai (1988), *The Moral Dimension. Toward a New Economics*, New York: Free Press.

Fama, Eugene F. and Michael C. Jensen (1983), 'Separation of Ownership and Control', *Journal of Law and Economics*, **26**, 301–51.

Faulhaber, Gerald R. and William J. Baumol (1988), 'Economists as Innovators', *Journal of Economic Literature*, **30** (2), 577–600.

Fehr, Ernst, Georg Kirchsteiger and Arno Riedl (1993), 'Does Fairness

Prevent Market Clearing? An Experimental Investigation', *Quarterly Journal of Economics*, **108**, (May), 437–60.

Festinger, Leon (1957), *A Theory of Cognitive Dissonance*, Stanford: Stanford University Press.

Fischhoff, Baruch (1982), 'Debiasing', in Daniel Kahnemann; Paul Slovic and Amos Tversky (eds), *Judgement Under Uncertainty: Heuristics and Biases*, Cambridge: Cambridge University Press: 422–44.

Frank, Robert H. (1988), *Passions within Reason. The Strategic Role of the Emotions*, New York: Norton.

Frey, Bruno S. (1992a), *Economics as a Science of Human Behaviour*, Boston and Dordrecht: Kluwer.

Frey, Bruno S. (1992b), *Umweltökonomie*, Göttingen: Vandenhoeck and Ruprecht (3rd edn).

Frey, Bruno S. and Hannelore Weck-Hannemann (1984), 'The Hidden Economy as an "Unobserved" Variable', *European Economic Review*, **26**, 33–53.

Frey, Bruno S. and Iris Bohnet (1995), 'Institutions Affect Fairness: Experimental Investigations', *Journal of Institutional and Theoretical Economics*, **151** (June), 286–303.

Frey, Bruno S. and Iris Bohnet (1996), 'Cooperation, Communication and Communitarianism. An Experimental Approach', forthcoming in *Journal of Political Philosophy*.

Frey, Bruno S. and Klaus Foppa (1986), 'Human Behaviour: Possibilities Explain Action', *Journal of Economic Psychology*, **7**, 137–60.

Frey, Bruno S. and Reiner Eichenberger (1989), 'Anomalies and Institutions', *Journal of Institutional and Theoretical Economics*, **145** (September),423–37.

Frey, Bruno S. and Reiner Eichenberger (1993), 'American and European Economics and Economists', *Journal of Economic Perspectives*, **9** (1), Winter, 203–12.

Frey, Bruno S. and Reiner Eichenberger (1994), 'Economic Incentives Transform Psychological Anomalies', *Journal of Economic Behaviour and Organisation*, **23**, 215–34.

Frey, Bruno S. and Reiner Eichenberger (1997), 'Economists: First Semester, High Flyers, and UFOs', in 'Economic Science: An Art or An Asset?' Aldershot: Edward Elgar.

Frey, Bruno S. and Werner W. Pommerehne (1989), *Muses and Markets: Explorations in the Economics of the Arts*, Oxford: Blackwell.

Frey, Bruno S. and Werner W. Pommerehne (1993), 'On the Fairness of

Pricing – An Empirical Survey among the General Population', *Journal of Economic Behavior and Organization*, **20**, 295–307.

Friedman, Milton (1970), 'The Social Responsibility of Business is to Increase Its Profits', reprinted in T. Beauchamp and N. Bowie (eds), *Ethical Theory and Business*, Englewood Cliffs: Prentice Hall, 1988.

Furnham, Adrian and Alan Lewis (1986), *The Economic Mind. The Social Psychology of Economic Behaviour*, Baltimore and Brighton: Wheatsheaf Books, Harvester Press.

Gilad, Benjamin, Stanley Kaish and Peter D. Loeb (1987), 'Cognitive Dissonance and Utility Maximization', *Journal of Economic Behavior and Organization*, **8**, 61–73.

Goetze, David (1982), 'A Decentralized Mechanism for Siting Hazardous Waste Disposal Facilities', *Public Choice*, **39**, 361–70.

Goldthorp, John H., David Lockwood, Frank Bechhofer and Jennifer Platt (1968), *The Affluent Worker: Industrial Attitudes and Behavior*, Cambridge: Cambridge University Press.

Goodin, Robert E. (1980), 'Making Moral Incentives Pay', *Policy Sciences*, **12** (August), 131–46.

Gordon, David M. (1994), 'Bosses of Different Stripes: A Cross-National Perspective on Monitoring and Supervision', *American Economic Review, Papers and Proceedings*, **84** (May), 375–9.

Gouldner, Alvin Ward (1960), 'The Norm of Reciprocity: A Preliminary Statement', *American Sociological Review*, **25**, 161–78.

Graetz, Michael J. and Louis L. Wilde (1985), 'The Economics of Tax Compliance: Facts and Fantasy', *National Tax Journal*, **38** (September), 355–63.

Graetz, Michael J., Jennifer F. Reinganum and Louis L. Wilde (1986), 'The Tax Compliance Game: Toward an Interactive Theory of Law Enforcement', *Journal of Law, Economics and Organization*, **2**, 1–32.

Granovetter, Mark (1985), 'Economic Action and Social Structure: The Problem of Imbeddedness', *American Journal of Sociology*, **91**, 481–510.

Grasmick, Harold G. and Robert J. Bursik (1990), 'Conscience, Significant Others, and Rational Choice: Extending the Deterrence Model', *Law and Society Review*, **24**, 837–61.

Gross, Jan T. (1982), 'A Note on the Nature of Soviet Totalitarianism', *Soviet Studies* , **34** (July), 367–76.

Gruenberg, Barry (1980), 'The Happy Worker: Determinants of Job Satisfaction', *American Journal of Sociology*, **86**, 247–71.

Güth, Werner and Reinhard Tietz (1990), 'Ultimatum Bargaining Behaviour. A Survey and Comparison of Experimental Results', *Journal of Economic Psychology*, **11**, 417–49.

Güth, Werner, R. Schmittberger and B. Schwarze (1982), 'An Experimental Analysis of Ultimatum Bargaining', *Journal of Economic Behaviour and Organization*, **3**, 367–88.

Guzzo, Richard A. and Raymond A. Katzell (1987), 'Effects of Economic Incentives on Productivity: A Psychological View', in Haig R. Nalbantian (ed.), *Incentives, Cooperation and Risk Sharing*, Totowa, NJ: Rowman and Littlefield, 107–19.

Hahn, Robert W. (1989), 'Economic Prescriptions for Environmental Problems. How the Patients Followed the Doctor's Orders', *Journal of Economic Perspectives*, **3** (Spring), 95–114.

Hamilton, James T. (1993), 'Politics and Social Costs: Estimating the Impact of Collective Action on Hazardous Waste Facilities', *Rand Journal of Economics*, **24** (Spring), 101–25.

Hansmann, Henry B. (1987), 'The Economics and Ethics of Markets for Human Organs', *Journal of Health Politics, Policy and Law*, **14**, 57–85.

Hart, Oliver and Bengt Holmström (1987), 'The Theory of Contracts', in Truman Bewley (ed.), *Advances in Economic Theory*, Cambridge: Cambridge University Press.

Hawkins, Keith and John M. Thomas (eds) (1984), *Enforcing Regulation*, Boston: Kluwer.

Hayek, Friedrich A. (1978), 'Competition as Discovery Procedure', in Friedrich A. Hayek, *New Studies in Philosophy, Politics, Economics and the History of Ideas*, London: Routledge and Kegan, 119–30.

Hayes, Samuel H. (1967), 'A Military View of Selective Service', in Sol Tax (ed.), *The Draft*, Chicago and London: University of Chicago Press, 7–22.

Hensher, David and Lester W. Johnson (1981), *Applied Discrete Choice Modelling*, London: Croom Helm.

Hess, Rudolf (1959), *Commandant at Auschwitz: Autobiography*, London: Weidenfeld and Nicholson.

Hirsch, Fred (1976), *The Social Limits to Growth*, Cambridge, MA: Harvard University Press.

Hirschman, Albert O. (1958), *The Strategy of Economic Development*, New Haven: Yale University Press.

Hirschman, Albert O. (1970), *Exit, Voice and Loyalty*, Cambridge, MA: Harvard University Press.

Hirschman, Albert O. (1977), *The Passions and the Interests. Political Arguments for Capitalism before its Triumph*, Princeton, NJ: Princeton University Press.

Hirschman, Albert O. (1982), *Shifting Involvements. Private Interests and Public Action*, Oxford: Martin Robertson.

Hirshleifer, Jack (1985), 'The Expanding Domain of Economics', *American Economic Review*, **75** (May), 53–68.

Hirst, Mark K. (1988), 'Intrinsic Motivation as Influenced by Task Interdependence and Goal Setting', *Journal of Applied Psychology*, **73** (1), 96–101.

Holmström, Bengt and Paul Milgrom (1990), 'Multi-Task Principle–Agent Analysis: Incentive Contracts, Asset Ownership and Job Design', *Journal of Law, Economics and Organization*, **7**, 24–52.

Horkheimer, Max (1952), *Zum Begriff der Vernunft*, Frankfurt: Klostermann.

Hosmer, David W. Jr. and Stanley Lemeshow (1989), *Applied Logistic Regression*, New York: John Wiley.

Hough, Douglas E. (1978), *The Market for Human Blood*, Lexington, MA: Heath.

Hume, David (1963), 'Of Independency of Parliament', *Essays. Moral, Political and Literary*, **1**, London: University Press.

Inglehart, Ronald (1981), 'Post-Materialism in an Environment of Insecurity', *American Political Science Review*, **75**, 880–900.

Institute of Economic Affairs (1973), *The Economics of Charity: Essays on the Comparative Economics and Ethics of Giving, Selling, with Applications to Blood*, London: Institute of Economic Affairs.

Ireland, Thomas R. and James V. Koch (1973), 'Blood and American Social Attitudes', in *The Economics of Charity*, London: Institute of Economic Affairs, 145–55.

Janowitz, Morris (1973), 'The Social Demography of the All-Volunteer Armed Force', *Annals of the American Academy of Political and Social Science*, **406** (March), 86–93.

Jencks, Christopher, Lauri Perman and Lee Rainwater (1988), 'What is a Good Job? A New Measure of Labor-Market Success', *American Journal of Sociology*, **93**, 1322–57.

Jensen, Michael C. (1992), 'Reputational Spillovers, Innovation, Licensing and Entry', *International Journal of Industrial Organization*, **10**, 193–212.

Johnson, James (1993), 'Is Talk Really Cheap? Prompting Conversation between Critical Theory and Rational Choice', *American Political Science Review*, **87**, 74–86.

Kagan, Robert A. and John T. Scholz (1984), 'The Criminology of Cooperation and Regulatory Enforcement Strategies' in Keith Hawkins and John M. Thomas (eds), *Enforcing Regulation*, Boston: Kluwer.

Kahn, Melvin L. and Carmi Schooler (1983), *Work and Personality*, Norwood NJ: Ablex.

Kahneman, Daniel, Jack Knetsch and Richard Thaler (1986a), 'Fairness as Constraint on Profit Seeking: Entitlements in the Market', *American Economic Review*, **76** (September), 728–41.

Kahneman, Daniel, Jack Knetsch and Richard Thaler (1986b), 'Fairness and the Assumption of Economics', *Journal of Business*, **59**, 285–300.

Kant, Immanuel (1795), *Zum Ewigen Frieden, Kants gesammelte Schriften*, Königliche Preussische Akademie der Wissenschaft (ed.), vol.8, Berlin and Leipzig (1923). Photomech. reproduction 1969.

Kazdin, Alan E. (1982), 'The Token Economy: A Decade Later', *Journal of Applied Behavior Analysis*, **15** (Autumn), 431–45.

Kazdin, Alan E. and R.R. Bootzin (1972), 'The Token Economy: An Evaluative Review', *Journal of Applied Behavior Analysis*, **5**, 343–98.

Kellet, Anthony (1982), *Combat Motivation: The Behavior of Soldiers in Battle*, Boston: Kluwer.

Kelman, H.C. (1969), 'Patterns of Personal Involvement in the National System: A Socio-psychological Analysis of Political Legitimacy', in J. Rosenau (ed.), *International Politics and Foreign Policy* (rev. edn), New York: Free Press.

Kelman, Steven (1981), *What Price Incentives? Economists and the Environment*, Boston: Auburn House.

Kelman, Steven (1987), *Making Public Policy: A Hopeful View of American Government*, New York: Basic Books.

Kelman, Steven (1992), 'Adversary and Cooperationist Institutions for Conflict Resolution in Public Policymaking', *Journal of Policy Analysis and Management*, **11**, 178–206.

Kemp, Ray (1992), *The Politics of Radioactive Waste Disposal*, Manchester: University Press.

Kendrick, John W. (1987), 'Group Financial Incentives: An Evaluation', in Haig R. Nalbantian (ed.) *Incentives, Cooperation and Risk Sharing*, Totowa, NJ: Rowman and Littlefield, 120–36.

Kinsey, Karyl A. (1992), 'Deterrence and Alienation Effects of IRS Enforcement: An Analysis of Survey Data', in Joel Slemrod (ed.),

Why People Pay Taxes. Tax Compliance and Enforcement, Ann Arbor: University of Michigan Press.

Kirchgässner, Gebhard (1991), *Homo Oeconomicus: Das ökonomische Modell individuellen Verhaltens und seine Anwendung in den Wirtschafts- und Sozialwissenschaften*, Tübingen: Mohr (Siebeck).

Kirchgässner, Gebhard (1992), 'Towards a Theory of Low-Cost Decisions', *European Journal of Political Economy*, **8**, 305–20.

Kirchgässner, Gebhard and Werner W. Pommerehne (1993), 'Low-cost Decisions as a Challenge to Public Choice', *Public Choice*, **77** (September), 107–15.

Klamer, Arjo (1995), 'The Value of Culture', *Boekmancahier*, **7** (25), 298–310.

Kliemt, Hartmut (1986), 'The Veil of Insignificance', *European Journal of Political Economy*, **2/3**, 333–44.

Kohn, Alfie (1993a), *Punished by Rewards: The Trouble with Gold Stars, Incentive Plans, A's Praise, and Other Bribes*, Boston: Houghton Mifflin.

Kohn, Alfie (1993b), 'Why Incentive Plans Cannot Work', *Harvard Business Review*, **5** (September/October), 54–63.

Kornhauser, Arthur W. (1965), *Mental Health of the Industrial Worker: A Detroit Study*, New York: Wiley.

Kruglanski, Arie W. (1978), 'Endogenous Attribution and Intrinsic Motivation', in Mark Lepper and David Greene (eds), *The Hidden Costs of Reward: New Perspectives on the Psychology of Human Motivation*, Hillsdale, NY: Erlbaum, 93–118.

Kunreuther, Howard and Douglas Easterling (1990), 'Are Risk–Benefit Tradeoffs Possible in Siting Hazardous Facilities?' *American Economic Review*, **80** (May), 295–9.

Kunreuther, Howard and Paul Portney (1991), 'Wheel of Misfortune: A Lottery Auction Mechanism for the Siting of Noxious Facilities', *Journal of Energy Engineering*, **117**, 125–32.

Kuran, Timur (1989), 'Sparks and Prairie Fires: A Theory of Unanticipated Political Revolution', *Public Choice*, **61** (1), 41–74.

Lågergren, Mårten (project leader) and Lena Lundh (1984), *Time to Care: A Report prepared for the Swedish Secretariat for Future Studies*, Oxford: Pergamon Press.

Lane, Robert (1991), *The Market Experience*, Cambridge: Cambridge University Press.

Lawler, Edward E. and Paul W. O'Gara (1967), 'The Effects of Inequity Produced by Underpayment on Work Output, Work Quality and

Attitudes Toward Work', *Journal of Applied Psychology*, **51** (October), 403–10.

Lazear, Edward P. (1991), 'Labor Economics and the Psychology of Organizations', *Journal of Economic Perspectives*, **5** (Spring), 89–110.

Lazear, Edward P. and Sherwin Rosen (1981), 'Rank-Order Tournaments as Optimum Labour Contracts', *Journal of Political Economy*, **89** (5), 841–64.

Lea, Stephen E.G., Roger M. Tarpy and Paul Webley (1987), *The Individual and the Economy. A Survey of Economic Psychology*, Cambridge: Cambridge University Press.

Leibenstein, Harvey (1976), *Beyond Economic Man. A New Foundation for Microeconomics*, Cambridge MA: Harvard University Press.

Leibenstein, Harvey and Shlomo Maital (1994), 'The Organizational Foundation of X-Inefficiency. A Game-Theoretical Interpretation of Argyris-Model of Organizational Learning', *Journal of Economic Behavior and Organization*, **23**, 251–68.

Lepper, Mark R. and David Greene (eds) (1978), *The Hidden Costs of Reward: New Perspectives on the Psychology of Human Motivation*, Hillsdale, NY: Erlbaum.

Lewis, Alan (1982), *The Psychology of Taxation*, Oxford: Blackwell.

Liddell Hart B.H. (1982), 'Why Don't We Learn from History?' in Martin Anderson (ed.), *The Military Draft. Selected Readings on Conscription*, Stanford: Hoover Institution Press, 35–45.

Lightman, Ernie S. (1981), 'Continuity in Social Policy Behaviors: The Case of Voluntary Blood Donorship', *Journal of Social Policy*, **10** (January), 53–97.

Lind, E. Allan and Tom R. Tyler (1988), *The Social Psychology of Procedural Justice*, New York and London: Plenum Press.

Lindenberg, Siegwart (1985), 'Rational Choice and Sociological Theory: New Pressures on Economics as a Social Science', *Journal of Institutional and Theoretical Economics*, **141**, 244–55.

Lindenberg, Siegwart (1988), 'Contractual Relations and Weak Solidarity: the Behavioral Basis of Restraint on Gain-Maximization', *Journal of Institutional and Theoretical Economics*, **144**, 39–58.

Linnerooth-Bayer, Joanne, Benjamin Davy, Andrea Faast and Kevin Fitzgerald (1994), *Hazardous Waste Cleanup and Facility Siting in Central Europe: The Austrian Case*, Laxenburg: International Institute for Applied Systems Analysis.

Machina, Mark J. (1987), 'Choice Under Uncertainty: Problems Solved and Unsolved', *Journal of Economic Perspectives*, **1** (1), 121–54.

Magat, Wesley A. and Kip W. Viscusi (1990), 'Effectiveness of the EPA's Regulatory Enforcement: The Case of Industrial Effluent Standards', *Journal of Law and Economics*, **33** (2), 331–60.

Maital, Shlomo (1988), 'Novelty, Comfort, and Pleasure: Inside the Utility-Function Black Box', in P.J. Albanese (ed.), *Psychological Foundations of Economic Behavior*, New York: Praeger, 1–34.

Mansbridge, Jane (1994), 'Public Spirit in Political Systems', in Henry J. Aaron, Thomas E. Mann and Timothy Taylor (eds), *Values and Public Policy*, Washington: Brookings Institution, 146–72.

Marcuse, Herbert (1965), 'Industrialization and Capitalism', *New Left Review* (March/April), 3–17.

Mayer, Thomas (1993), *Truth versus Precision in Economics*, Aldershot: Edward Elgar.

McClelland, D.C. (1961), *The Achieving Society*, Free Press: New York.

McGraw, K.O. (1978), 'The Detrimental Effects of Reward on Performance: A Literature Review and a Prediction Model', in Mark R. Lepper and David Greene (eds), *The Hidden Costs of Reward: New Perspectives of Human Behaviour*, Hillsdale, NY: Erlbaum, 33–60.

McKenzie, Richard B. and Gordon Tullock (1975), *The New World of Economics* (2nd edn), Homewood, Il: Irwin.

Menchik, Paul and Burt Weisbrod (1987), 'Volunteer Labor Supply', *Journal of Public Economics*, **32**, 159–83.

Michelman, F.I. (1967), 'Property, Utility and Fairness: Comments on the Ethical Foundations of "Just Compensation" Laws', *Harvard Law Review*, **80**, 1165–258.

Mill, John S. (1861) 'Considerations on Representative Government', *Essays on Politics and Society*, 19 of the Collected Works, London: Forum Books, [1861], 1958.

Miller, G. Tyler (1990), *Living in the Environment* (6th edn), Belmont, CA: Wadsworth.

Minford, Patrick (1992), *Rational Expectations Macroeconomics: An Introductory Handbook*, Oxford and Cambridge: Blackwell.

Mintzberg, Henry (1975), 'The Manager's Job: Folklore and Fact', *Harvard Business Review*, **53** (July–August), 49–61.

Mitchell, Robert C. and Richard T. Carson (1986), 'Property Rights, Protest, and the Siting of Hazardous Waste Facilities', *American Economic Review*, Papers and Proceedings, **76** (May), 285–90.

Mitchell, Robert C. and Richard T. Carson (1989), *Using Surveys to Value Public Goods: The Contingent Valuation Method*, Baltimore: Johns Hopkins Press.

Montesquieu, Charles Louis (1749), *De l'esprit des lois*, vol. XX, Paris: Garnier.

Mortimer, Jeylan T. (1979), *Changing Attitudes toward Work: Highlights of the Literature*, New York: Pergamon.

Mueller, Dennis C. (1995), *Constitutional Economics*, Cambridge: Cambridge University Press.

Musgrave, Richard A. (1981), 'The Leviathan cometh – or does he?', in Helen F. Ladd and T. Nicolaus Tideman (eds), *Tax and Expenditure Limitations*, Washington DC: Urban Institute Press, 73–120.

Nalbantian, Haig R. (1987), *Incentives, Cooperation, and Risk Sharing. Economic and Psychological Perspectives on Employment Contracts*, Totowa, NJ: Rowman and Littlefield.

Neiman, Max (1989), 'Government Directed Change of Every Day Life: The Case of Home Energy Use', *Western Political Quarterly*, **42**, 365–89.

Neubourg de, Chris and Maarten Vendrik (1994), 'An Extended Rationality Model of Social Norms in Labour Supply', *Journal of Economic Psychology*, **15**, 93–126.

North, Douglass C. (1990), *Institutions, Institutional Change, and Economic Performance*, Cambridge: Cambridge University Press.

O'Hare, Michael (1977), 'Not On My Block You Don't: Facility Siting and the Strategic Importance of Compensation, *Public Policy*, **25**, 409–58.

O'Hare, Michael, Lawrence Bacow and Debra Sanderson (1983), *Facility Siting and Public Opposition*, New York: Van Nostrand Reinhold.

O'Sullivan, Arthur (1993), 'Voluntary Auctions for Noxious Facilities: Incentives to Participate and the Efficiency of Siting Decisions', *Journal of Environmental Economics and Management*, **25**, 12–26.

Oberholzer-Gee, Felix, Bruno S. Frey, Albert Hart and Werner W. Pommerehne (1995), 'Panik, Protest und Paralyse. Eine empirische Untersuchung über nukleare Endlager in der Schweiz', *Schweiz. Zeitschrift für Volkswirtschaft und Statistik*, **131** (2), 147–77.

OECD (1989), *Economic Instruments for Environmental Protection*, Paris: Organization for Economic Cooperation and Development.

Opaluch, James J., Stephen K. Swallow, Thomas Weaver, Christopher W. Wessells and Dennis Wichelns (1993), 'Evaluating Impacts from Noxious Facilities: Including Public Preferences in Current Siting

Mechanisms', *Journal of Environmental Economics and Management*, **24**, 41–59.

Osterloh, Margit, Simon Grand and Regine Tiemann (1994), 'Organisationales Lernen: Was kann die ökonomische Theorie dazu beitragen?' in Hans Nutzinger (ed.), Schriften des Vereins für Socialpolitik. Berlin: Duncker und Humblot, 37–76.

Osterman, Paul (1994), 'Supervision, Discretion, and Work Organization', *American Economic Review*, **84** (2) May, 380–84.

Ostrom, Elinor (1990), *Governing the Commons: The Evolution of Institutions for Collective Action*, Cambridge: Cambridge University Press.

Oswalt, Robert M. (1977), 'A Review of Blood Donor Motivation and Procurement', *Transfusion*, **17**, 124–44.

Parkin, Sara (1989), *Green Parties. An International Guide*, London: Heretic Books.

Parsons, Talcott (1967), 'Some Reflections on the Place of Force in the Social Process', in Talcott Parsons (ed.), *Sociological Theory and Modern Society*, New York: Free Press.

Peltzman, Sam (1975), 'The Effects of Automobile Safety Regulation', *Journal of Political Economy*, **83** (4), 677–726.

Petersen, Trond (1993), 'The Economics of Organization: The Principal–Agent Relationship', *Acta Sociologica*, **36**, 277–93.

Peterson, Steven, George Hoffer and Edward Millner (1995), 'Are Drivers of Air-Bag-Equipped Cars More Aggressive? A Test of the Offsetting Behavior Hypothesis', *Journal of Law and Economics*, **38** (October), 251–64.

Pittman, Thane S. and Jack F. Heller (1987), 'Social Motivation', *Annual Review of Psychology*, **38**, 461–89.

Pommerehne, Werner W. and Bruno S. Frey (1993), 'The Effects of Tax Administration on Tax Morale', unpublished manuscript, Department of Economics, University of the Saar.

Pommerehne, Werner W., Friedrich Schneider, Guy Gilbert and Bruno S. Frey (1984), 'Concordia Discors: Or: What do Economists Think?', *Theory and Decision*, **16**, 251–308.

Portney, Paul R. (1991), *Siting Hazardous Waste Treatment Facilities: The NIMBY Syndrome*, New York: Auburn House.

Poterba, James M. and Kim S. Rueben (1994), *The Distribution of Public Sector Wage Premia. New Evidence Using Quarterly Regression Methods*, Cambridge MA: NBER Working Paper No. 4734.

Pyle, D.J. (1990), 'The Economics of Taxpayer Compliance', *Journal of Economic Surveys*, **5**, 163–98.

Rawls, John (1971), *A Theory of Justice*, Cambridge, MA: Harvard University Press.

Reber, Ralph W. and Gloria van Gilder (1982), *Behavioral Insights for Supervision*, Englewood Cliffs, NJ: Prentice Hall.

Renn, Ortwin, Thomas Webler and Hans Kastenholz (1996), 'Procedural and Substantive Fairness in Landfill Siting', *Risk, Health, Safety and Environment*, **7** (2), 145–68.

Ribeaux, Peter and Stephen E. Poppleton (1978), *Psychology of Work: an Introduction*, London: Macmillan.

Richardson, F.M. (1978), *Fighting Spirit: A Study of Psychological Factors in War*, London: Cooper.

Roberts, Russel D. and Michael J. Wolkoff (1988), 'Improving the Quality and Quantity of Whole Blood Supply: Limits to Voluntary Arrangements', *Journal of Health Politics, Policy and Law*, **13** (Spring), 167–78.

Robertson, Dennis H. (1956), 'What does the Economist Economize?' in *Economic Commentaries*, London: Staples.

Rodman, John (1983), 'Four Forms of Ecological Conciousness Reconsidered', in Scherer, Donald and Thomas Attig (eds), *Ethics and the Environment*, Englewood Cliffs: Prentice Hall.

Ross, Thomas W. (1988), *Raising an Army: A Positive Theory of Military Recruitment*, Stanford Hoover Institute Working Paper in Economics: 88–46.

Roth, Alvin E. (1995), 'Bargaining Experiments', in John Kagel and Alvin E. Roth (eds), *Handbook of Experimental Economics*, Princeton: Princeton University Press, 253–348.

Roth, Jeffrey A., John T. Scholz and Ann Dryden Witte (eds) (1989), *Taxpayer Compliance*, Philadelphia: University of Pennsylvania Press.

Rotter, Julian (1966), 'Generalized Expectancies for Internal versus External Control of Reinforcement', *Psychological Monographs*, **80** (1), no. 609.

Sally, David (1995), 'Conversation and Cooperation in Social Dilemmas. A Meta-Analysis of Experiments from 1958 to 1992', *Rationality and Society*, **7** (1), 58–92.

Sappington, David E.M. (1991), 'Incentives in Principal–Agent Relationships', *Journal of Economic Perspectives*, **5** (Spring), 45–66.

Sarat, Amos (1975), 'Support for the Legal System', *American Politics Quarterly*, **3**, 3–24.

Schelling, Thomas C. (1978), 'Egonomics, or the Art of Self-Management', *American Economic Review*', **68** (May), 290–94.

Schelling, Thomas C. (1980), 'The Intimate Contest for Self-Command', *Public Interest*, **60** (Summer), 94–118.

Schlicht, Ekkehart (1979), 'The Transition to Labour Management as a Gestalt Switch', *Gestalt Theory*, **1**, 54–67.

Schlicht, Ekkehart (1990), 'Social Psychology: A Review Article', *Journal of Institutional and Theoretical Economics*, **146**, 355–62.

Schmölders, Günter (1960), *Steuern und Staatsausgaben in der öffentlichen Meinung der Bundesrepublik*, Köln/Opladen: Westdeutscher Verlag.

Schmölders, Günter (1970), 'Survey Research in Public Finance: A Behavioural Approach to Fiscal Policy', *Public Finance*, **25**, 300–306.

Schoemaker, Paul J. (1982), 'The Expected Utility Model: Its Variants, Purposes, Evidence and Limitations', *Journal of Economic Literature*, **20** (June), 529–63.

Schultz, Kenneth A. and Barry R. Weingast (1994), 'The Democratic Advantage: The Institutional Sources of State Power in International Competition', Mimeo, Stanford University.

Schumpeter, Joseph A. (1936), *The Theory of Economic Development*, Cambridge: Harvard University Press.

Schumpeter, Joseph A. (1942), *Capitalism, Socialism and Democracy*, New York: Harper.

Schwartz, Richard D. and Sonya Orleans (1967), 'On Legal Sanctions', *University of Chicago Law Review*, **34**, 282–300.

Scitovsky, Tibor (1976), *The Joyless Economy: An Inquiry into Human Satisfaction and Consumer Dissatisfaction*, Oxford: Oxford University Press.

Scitovsky, Tibor (1981), 'The Desire for Excitement in Modern Society', *Kyklos*, **34**, 3–13.

Scott, W.E., Jiing-Lih Farh and Philip M. Podsakoff (1988), 'The Effects of "Intrinsic" and "Extrinsic" Reinforcement Contingencies on Task Behavior', *Organizational Behavior and Human Decision Processes*, **41**, 405–25.

Selten, Reinhard and Reinhard Tietz (1980), 'Zum Selbstverständnis der experimentellen Wirtschaftsforschung im Umkreis von Heinz Sauermann', *Journal of Institutional and Theoretical Economics*, **136**, 12–27.

Sen, Amartya K. (1977), 'Rational Fools: A Critique of the Behavioral Foundations of Economic Theory', *Philosophy and Public Affairs*, **6**, 317–44.

Sen, Amartya K. (1982), *Choice, Welfare and Measurement*, Oxford: Blackwell.

Sen, Amartya K. (1987), *On Ethics and Economics*, Oxford: Blackwell.

Shapiro, Carl and Joseph E. Stiglitz (1984), 'Equilibrium Unemployment as a Worker Discipline Device', *American Economic Review*, **74** (June), 433–44.

Sigmon, E. Brent (1987), 'Achieving a Negotiated Compensation Agreement in Siting: The MRS Case', *Journal of Policy Analysis and Management*, **6** (2), 170–79.

Simon, Herbert A. (1957), *Models of Man*, New York: Wiley.

Simon, Herbert A. (1982), *Models of Bounded Rationality*, Cambridge, MA: MIT Press.

Simon, Herbert A. (1991), 'Organizations and Markets', *Journal of Economic Perspectives*, **5** (Spring), 25–44.

Simonton, Dean Keith (1994), *Greatness. Who Makes History and Why*, New York and London: Guilford Press.

Singer, Peter (1973), 'Altruism and Commerce: A Defence of Titmuss against Arrow', *Philosophy and Public Affairs*, **2** (Spring), 312–20.

Skinner, J. and Slemrod, Joel (1985), 'An Economic Perspective on Tax Evasion', *National Tax Journal*, **38**, 345–53.

Slemrod, Joel (ed.) (1992), *Why People Pay Taxes. Tax Compliance and Enforcement*, Ann Arbor: University of Michigan Press.

Slovic, Paul, James Flynn and Mark Layman (1991), 'Perceived Risk, Trust, and the Politics of Nuclear Waste', *Science*, **254**, 1603–7.

Smith, Adam (1776), *An Inquiry into the Nature and Causes of the Wealth of Nations*, Reprinted 1981, London: Deut & Sane Ltd.

Smith, Kent W. (1992), 'Reciprocity and Fairness: Positive Incentives for Tax Compliance', in Joel Slemrod (ed.), *Why People Pay Taxes. Tax Compliance and Enforcement*, Ann Arbor: University of Michigan Press, 223–50.

Solow, Robert S. (1971), 'Blood and Thunder', *Yale Law Journal*, **80**, 170–83.

Staw, Barry M. (1976), *Intrinsic and Extrinsic Motivation*, Morristown, NJ: General Learning Press.

Stigler, George J. (1984), *The Intellectual and the Marketplace*, Cambridge, MA: Harvard University Press.

Stigler, George J. and Gary S. Becker (1977), 'De Gustibus Non Est Disputandum', *American Economic Review*, **67** (March), 76–90.

Stiglitz, Joseph, E. (1987), 'The Design of Labor Contracts: The Economics of Incentives and Risk Sharing', in Haig R. Nalbantian (ed.),

Incentives, Cooperation and Risk Sharing, Totowa, NJ: Rowman and Littlefield, 47–68.

Stiglitz, Joseph E. (ed.) (1991), 'Symposium on Organizations and Economics', *Journal of Economic Perspectives*, **5** (Spring), 15–88.

Strümpel, Burkhard (1969), 'The Contribution of Survey Research to Public Finance', in Alan T. Peacock (ed.), *Quantitative Analysis in Public Finance*, Praeger: New York, 13–38.

Stuart, Charles E. (1984), 'Welfare Costs per Dollar of Additional Tax Revenue in the United States', *American Economic Review*, **74** (3), 352–62.

Sugden, Robert (1989), 'Spontaneous Order', *Journal of Economic Perspectives*, **3**, 85–98.

Tax, Sol (ed.) (1967), *The Draft*, Chicago and London: University of Chicago Press.

Thaler, Richard H. (1980), 'Toward a Positive Theory of Consumer Choice', *Journal of Economic Behavior and Organization*, **1** (March), 39–60.

Thaler, Richard H. (1987), 'The Psychology of Choice and the Assumption of Economics', in Alvin E. Roth (ed.), *Laboratory Experimentation in Economics*, Cambridge: Cambridge University Press, 99–130.

Thaler, Richard H. (1992), *The Winner's Curse. Paradoxes and Anomalies of Economic Life*, New York: Free Press.

Thaler, Richard H. and H.M. Shefrin (1981), 'An Economic Theory of Self-Control', *Journal of Political Economy*, **89** (April), 392–406.

Thibaut, John W. and Laurens Walker (1976), *Procedural Justice: A Psychological Analyis*, Hillsdale, NJ.

Thorndike, E.L. (1933), 'An Experimental Study of Rewards', Teachers College Contributions to Education no. 580.

Titmuss, Richard M. (1970), *The Gift Relationship*, London: Allen and Unwin.

Tullock, Gordon (1974), 'Does Punishment Deter Crime?', *Public Interest*, **36** (Summer), 103–11.

Tyler, Tom R. (1990), *Why People Obey the Law*, New Haven and London: Yale University Press.

Tyler, Tom R. and Kathleen M. McGraw (1986), 'Ideology and the Interpretation of Personal Experience: Procedural Justice and Political Quiescence', *Journal of Social Issues*, **42** (2), 115–28.

Upton, W., II (1973), 'Altruism, Attribution and Intrinsic Motivation in the Recruitment of Blood Donors', in *Selected Readings in Donor Motivation and Recruitment*, vol. III, ed. American Red Cross.

Vari, Anna, Patricia Reagan-Cirincione and Jeryl L. Mumpower (1993), *LLRW Disposal Facility Siting Processes in the United States, Western Europe, and Canada: Final Report for the New York State Energy Research and Development Authority*, Albany: Energy Research and Development Authority.

Veljanovski Cento G. (1984), 'The Economics of Regulatory Enforcement', in Keith Hawkins and John M. Thomas (eds), *Enforcing Regulations*, Boston: Kluwer, 171–88.

Viscusi, W. Kip (1984), *Regulating Consumer Product Safety*, Washington and London: American Enterprise Institute for Public Policy Research.

Vogel, Ezra T. (1965), 'From Friendship to Comradeship: The Change in Personal Relations in Communist Societies', *China Quarterly*, **21**, 46–70.

Wallace, Edgar L. (1985), 'The Case for National Blood Policy', in Ross D. Eckert (ed.), *Securing a Safer Blood Supply: Two Views*, Washington and London: American Enterprise Institute for Public Policy Research, 85–153.

Walster, Elaine, William G. Walster and Ellen Berscheid (1977), *Equity: Theory and Research*, Boston: Allyn and Bacon.

Warr, Peter (1987), *Work, Unemployment and Mental Health*, Oxford: Clarendon Press.

Weber, Max (1920–21), 'Die protestantische Ethik und der Geist des Kapitalismus', in Max Weber, *Gesammelte Aufsätze zur Religionssoziologie*, Tübingen: Mohr (Siebeck).

Weck-Hannemann, Hannelore (1994), 'Die politische Ökonomie der Umweltpolitik', in Rainer Bartel and Franz Hackl (eds), *Einführung in die Umweltpolitik*, München: Franz Vahlen, 101–17.

Weinstein, Neil D. (1980), 'Unrealistic Optimism About Future Life Events', *Journal of Personality and Social Psychology*, **39**, 806–20.

Weisbrod, Burt A. (1988), *The Nonprofit Economy*, Cambridge, MA: Harvard University Press.

Whitaker, Gordon P. (1980), 'Coproduction: Citizen Participation in Service Delivery', *Public Administration Review*, **42**, 240–46.

Wicke, Lutz (1991), 'Economic Responses to Global Warming: Prospects for Cooperative Approaches: Comments', in Rudiger Dornbusch and James M. Poterba (eds), *Global Warming: Economic Policy Responses*, Cambridge, MA and London: MIT Press, 229–31.

Wiersma, Uco J. (1992), 'The Effects of Extrinsic Rewards on Intrinsic Motivation: A Meta-Analysis', *Journal of Occupational and Organizational Psychology*, **65**, 101–14.

Williamson, Oliver E. (1975), *Markets and Hierarchies: Analysis and Antitrust Implications*, New York: Free Press.

Williamson, Oliver E. (1983), 'Credible Commitments: Using Hostages to Support Exchange', *American Economic Review*, **73** (September), 519–40.

Williamson, Oliver E. (1985), *The Economic Institutions of Capitalism, Firms, Markets, Relational Contradicting*, New York: Free Press.

Williamson, Oliver E. (1993), 'Calculativeness, Trust and Economic Organization', *Journal of Law and Economics*, **36**, 453–86.

Yankelovich, Daniel and John Immerwahr (1984), 'The Work Ethic and Economic Vitality', in Michael L. Wachter and Susan M. Wachter (eds), *Removing Obstacles to Economic Growth*, Philadelphia: University of Pennsylvania Press, 144–70.

Young, H. Peyton (1994), *Equity – in Theory and Practice*, Princeton: University Press.

Author index

Subject index